Journey to
Softness

Also by Mark Rashid

Considering the Horse

A Good Horse Is Never a Bad Color

Horses Never Lie

Life Lessons from a Ranch Horse

Horsemanship Through Life

Big Horses, Good Dogs, and Straight Fences

A Life with Horses

Whole Heart, Whole Horse

Out of the Wild

Finding the Missed Path

Journey to
Softness

In Search of Feel and
Connection with the Horse

Mark Rashid

Foreword by Skip Ewing

TRAFALGAR SQUARE
North Pomfret, Vermont

First published in 2016 by
Trafalgar Square Books
North Pomfret, Vermont 05053

Disclaimer of Liability

Library of Congress Cataloging-in-Publication Data

Names: Rashid, Mark, author.
Title: A journey to softness : in search of feel and connection with the
    horse / Mark Rashid ; foreword by Skip Ewing.
Description: North Pomfret, Vermont : Trafalgar Square Books, 2016.
Identifiers: LCCN 2015031434 | ISBN 9781570767586 (paperback)
Subjects: LCSH: Horses--Training. | Horses--Behavior. | Horses--Psychol-
ogy. | Human-animal relationships. | BISAC: SPORTS & RECREATION /
Equestrian.
Classification: LCC SF287 .R2825 2016 | DDC 636.1/0835--dc23 LC record
available at http://lccn.loc.gov/2015031434

Cover photograph by Fall River Productions (info@fallriverproductions.com)
Book design by Laury Eddlemon
Cover design by RM Didier
Typefaces: Gotham, Helvetica Neue
Printed in the United States of America
10 9 8

For Declan, Jack, and Brinley

Contents

Foreword

Gratitude.

For the fact that you're reading this. For the fact that you may have chosen to ask the question, "How can I be even more skillful for my horse, any horse, every horse?" or perhaps "What might be here that opens the door of greater understanding, not just of horses, but of others . . . of myself?"

Gratitude.

For the journey you've already taken and the myriad decisions that may have led you to pick up this book; to watch, listen, learn, practice, care, try, refine, try again, teach, train, try yet again, and perhaps even transform habits and ways of thinking that no longer serve your relationships well, including the relationship you have with yourself.

Gratitude.

For the long history of effort leading to the heart and intention behind the words in this book and the many others my friend Mark Rashid has written.

Friend? I meant brother.

Gratitude.

For the offer to be involved with so many hearts, so many horses, and so many humans on so many levels.

Gratitude.

To all of you, for your willingness to reconsider the horse, again, and again, and again.

Gratitude.

I believe it's the best place to begin, an even better place to end, and a good way to assure that every ending is an even more skillful beginning.

As a friend of mine once wrote with me, "If you got it right more times than you got it wrong . . . you got it right."

Friend? I meant brother.

With great confidence that you know the spirit in which this was written,

Skip Ewing, Singer and Songwriter

Preface

Very early on, as I began working on the outline for this book, I realized that one of the main concepts I wanted to share was the fact that the development of softness truly is a journey—one with a beginning and a middle, but not necessarily an end. One of the other concepts I wanted to try to impart is the fact that if we're not working on softness in everything we do, achieving it when we are with our horses is going to be considerably more difficult.

I asked a few friends, all with different backgrounds, from different walks of life, and from different parts of the country, if they would be willing to share some thoughts on how the practice of softness has helped them in their respective occupations, as well as with their horsemanship. Many of them were kind enough to jot down their ideas on the subject, and these can be found throughout this book as "Reflections from My Friends." My thanks to all who contributed!

Mark Rashid
Estes Park, Colorado

There is *strength*
in muscle, but
power in softness.

—*Mark Rashid*

Powerful 1
Softness

Dwight and I hadn't been on horseback very long when we reached the top of a small mesa and looked down into the valley below, green with new spring grass and bathed in the yellow glow of sunrise. The valley was maybe a half-mile long and two hundred yards wide, and in it were a handful of horses. One looked to be black or very dark brown, one was an Appaloosa, two were gray, and three were sorrel. One of the sorrels had what appeared to be a new foal running at its side.

"Is that her?" I asked.

Dwight shifted in his saddle. "I don't think so."

"No?" I asked. "She's got a foal, and I doubt there were any other pregnant mares out here."

He tipped his weathered cowboy hat back and scratched his forehead. "No." He readjusted his hat. "I think she was a bay."

"A bay?"

"Or brown."

"You don't know what color she was?"

"It was dark."

"The horse?"

"I think so. But the sale was at night, so it was dark out."

He squinted down into the valley and watched the sorrel with the baby. "And it was over a week ago. I'm pretty sure she weren't no sorrel."

"Pretty sure?"

"Well, I did buy two sorrels," he said, still looking at the small herd below us. "But they was geldings. The mare was a bay . . . or brown . . . I think."

Satisfied, at least to some extent, that the mare we had come to find (and that, at Dwight's suggestion, we would take off the 3,500-acre pasture on which our ranch horses had wintered) was not with the band we were currently gazing upon, we turned our horses and continued on our way.

The excursion that morning had begun a couple of days earlier when I received a call from Dwight about some horses he had bought the weekend before. Dwight had made a trip up to Minnesota that weekend to visit friends and family, and while there, took a little side trip to a horse sale. Saddle horses were going pretty cheap, so he had taken it upon himself to buy a few head that he figured I might be able to use at the guest ranch where I was foreman.

Dwight, an excellent and lifelong stockman, had a good eye for both cattle and horses. He also had a heart as big as Montana; if there were a way to help someone, especially a friend, he would do it without hesitation. In this case, he knew I was going to be short some horses for the upcoming season and so had decided to "help" by picking up a few for me. Details— where the horses would go once he bought them, were they rideable, did they have some kind of communicable disease that could possibly infect every horse on the place—just weren't that important.

So, when he called to tell me he had bought a few horses for the ranch, and then told me he thought they were all healthy and had turned them in with our herd out on the pasture, I wasn't too concerned. Of course, I hadn't actually asked him to buy any horses for us and I had no idea what these horses looked like. The fact that he also seemed to be having trouble remembering what they looked like was a little troubling, as not all of the horses on the pasture belonged to the ranch. Some, about fifteen head or so, belonged to other folks from the area who also pastured their horses there during the winter.

There was a very good chance that we could accidentally take the wrong horse, which would open up a whole other can of worms.

At any rate, when Dwight called, he told me that he was pretty sure one of the horses he bought (the only mare) was pregnant, and he was just as sure that she was not more than a week or so away from foaling when he put her and the others in the pasture.

"I just got to thinking," he said. "We may want to go out and get her. Maybe bring her up to the ranch so she can foal out up there."

"You bought us a pregnant mare?"

"She was pretty cheap," he happily replied. "Besides, you get a two-for-one!"

"But we don't have a place for a mare and a . . ."

"And while we're down there, I'll try to pick out the others I bought for you. I think they'll work out real good for your outfit."

"You'll try to pick them out?" I remember asking, making an effort to hide the fatigue I was beginning to feel at the thought of all the extra work it was looking like his generosity was going to generate.

"Yeah," he said, cheerfully. "It was dark when I turned them into the pasture, so I'm not real sure what they look like."

So there we were, spending the better part of the day riding a big circle on 3,500 acres, looking for a mare I'd never seen that might be bay or dark brown, that also might be pregnant.

By half past three that afternoon, some nine hours after Dwight and I first threw a leg over our saddle horses, we found ourselves back at the same mesa we'd started out on, looking at the same little band of horses down in the long, narrow valley below. We had eliminated the rest of the horses—I knew which ones we already owned, recognized the brands on ones we didn't, or concluded that the colors of the horses we found didn't match the colors of the horses he bought.

This time, however, as we looked down into the valley, we could see that the foal was no longer running beside the sorrel it had been with earlier that day, but rather, was next to what appeared to be a black horse.

"Well," Dwight shrugged, "that's got to be her."

We turned our horses down a small ravine and worked our way to the valley floor. It didn't take long to get to the small band. The mare was a nice-looking, very dark bay, refined, with what looked to be some Morgan in her. She had a kind eye and was spending all her time moving her baby, an equally dark little stud foal, away from two of the sorrel geldings. One of the geldings, a sixteen-hand, rawboned mustang-looking horse with a Roman nose and a white strip on his face, seemed fixated on getting to the foal. The other, a much smaller, stocky little fellow with no markings whatsoever, seemed more intent on following the bigger horse rather than going after the mare or baby.

The baby had most likely been born that morning, probably just before we arrived, and looked worn out; the geldings' constant attention had caused the mare to keep the baby moving nonstop. There was no telling how much rest, if any, the foal had managed to get since we had first seen it that morning running at the gelding's side, or how much, if any, it had been able to nurse.

"Looks like that gelding's trying to get at that baby," Dwight said as he moved his horse into position to cut off the gelding.

I moved toward the mare and began turning her and the baby back in the direction of the path Dwight and I had taken to get into the valley. Once at the top, we'd be able to make our way over to a large catch pen near where we'd parked the truck and trailer that morning, not more than a half-mile away.

The mare started up the path easily, but it was clear almost from the start that the baby wasn't going to be able to make the climb. As soon as the trail gained elevation, which was pretty much right away, the baby stalled out, then stopped. This, of course, stopped the mare, who turned and nickered to the baby. But the already-exhausted youngster wouldn't, or couldn't, move.

"We'll need to take them around the long way," I said, bringing the mare off the path and back into the valley. "The little guy won't make this climb."

The "long way" was a narrow trail that followed the bottom of the mesa and then sloped gradually upward along its face to the south and, eventually, to the catch pen. It was about a half-mile farther than if we'd gone to the top of the mesa, but with the baby and our saddle horses as tired as they were, it was going to be easier to take the lower route.

I maneuvered the mare off the path to the top of the mesa and eased her forward along the lower trail, her baby walking wearily at her side. Dwight brought up the rear, with the two sorrel geldings trailing behind him. From time to time, Dwight would turn his horse and chase the two geldings back down the trail toward the valley, but inevitably, as soon as he turned back around to rejoin us, the geldings would charge up behind him once again.

On several occasions, the bigger gelding tried to pass both Dwight and me, but the trail was much too narrow and rocky for him to get around us, and he'd fall back in line. Finally, after nearly a half-hour and numerous stops to allow the baby to rest, we neared the flat ground that would take us to the catch pen. Dwight and I both knew that if the gelding got to that opening, he would easily be able to overtake us and get to the mare and baby.

So, with less than a hundred yards to go before the flat, Dwight turned and moved the two geldings almost all the way back down to the valley. While he was doing that, I took the mare and baby to the pen, opened the rusted metal gate, and moved them both quietly inside. Once that was done, my horse Buck and I headed for the truck to get a halter for the mare.

I had taken a halter with me that morning, tied to my saddle. We figured we'd just put it on the mare and pony her back to the trailer after we found her. But while Dwight's recollection of the mare's coloring was fairly correct, his recollection of how big she was had been a little off. He had apparently mixed up the sizes of the mare and the mustang-looking gelding, and the halter I brought was way too big for her.

I took a smaller halter from a pile in the bed of the truck, tossed the bigger one back, and returned to the catch pen about the same time Dwight came loping up the trail. When Buck and I reached the gate, I opened it and we went inside. I was closing the gate behind us as Dwight eased his horse to the pen fence and dismounted. The mare was quietly standing over the foal, who was lying on the ground fast asleep. I hated to disturb the little guy, as I'm sure it was the only rest he'd had all day. But it was early spring, and coming on dinnertime; we were going to be running out of daylight soon, and the ranch was some forty miles away.

Then, just as I began to ease Buck toward the mare so I could get her haltered, I heard an unearthly scream from the trail. I looked up in time to see the big sorrel gelding galloping toward us, head and tail high, mouth gaped open, bawling and squealing as he ran. He made a beeline for Dwight, then veered off at the last second, making a large circle in the meadow adjacent to the pen.

"That's enough of that," Dwight grunted, and without hesitation, jumped back in the saddle. He pulled the lariat from his saddle, shook out a loop, and began to swing it in a big arc over his head.

Then the second gelding suddenly appeared, loping up the trail and calling for his buddy, who by this time had finished his circle and was charging toward the pen's gate. He veered off again, making a smaller circle, then returned to the gate, where he slid to a stop, but not before crashing into it with his chest. He called frantically, shaking his head and stomping his feet.

The second gelding ran straight for the big red horse, stopping next to him. The big horse turned and bit him hard on the shoulder. By this time, Dwight had made his way around the pen and was moving in on the pair. He threw a loop at the horses, not so much to catch either one but rather, to get them to move away from the gate. Both bolted and immediately split up, the smaller horse moving to the east, the bigger one to the south.

As Dwight gathered his rope and began building another loop, the mustang-looking gelding wheeled back around and once again headed straight for the gate. This time, as Dwight began to swing the rope, the big gelding all but ignored it, breezed past Dwight and his horse, and jumped the gate just as pretty as you please, landing inside the pen.

I quickly turned toward the mare and saw that she had already roused her foal to his feet and was urging him forward while she shielded him from the gelding with her body. I moved Buck in front of the gelding, dropped the halter I was holding, and grabbed my rope. The gelding rushed past Buck and me as though we weren't there and headed for the mare and baby.

At this point, something quite extraordinary happened. As the gelding closed in on the mare, I watched her wheel her hindquarters toward him and kick him square in the chest, causing him to recoil a good fifteen feet. While the force the mare put into that kick was quite astounding, creating a shockwave I could feel from my position some thirty feet away, what was even more remarkable was something the mare did with her baby at the same time.

At the very moment she laid that powerful kick into the gelding's chest, the mare had also used her nose to ever-so-gently move her exhausted baby away from danger. It was an amazing feat of total body control. While her hindquarters seemed to harness all the strength of her body and hit the gelding with an accuracy and speed the like of which I have seldom seen, her front end was as soft as butter, guiding her foal to a safer place while barely touching him.

I didn't have much time to contemplate what I had just seen, however, as things that were only slightly out of hand just a few seconds earlier were beginning to get increasingly more "Western" as time went by. Outside the pen, Dwight had his hands full trying to chase the second horse away from the gate. The little gelding had tried to follow the bigger horse over it, but only managed to crash chest-first into it, nearly knocking it off its heavy metal hinges and springing the latch that held it closed. Startled by the metallic bang he made when he hit the gate, and Dwight's yelling and rope-swinging, the smaller gelding scrambled away from the gate and down the rail fence until he was roughly parallel with the bigger gelding, who was still inside the pen.

Meanwhile, the bigger gelding seemed momentarily stunned by the kick the mare had just administered and bolted for the far end of the pen, away from the mare and baby. His change of heart didn't last long, though, and after stopping for a second to touch noses with his newly arrived and frantic buddy, he turned his attention back to the mare and baby.

All of this activity had given me time to build a loop and allowed Dwight an opportunity to get himself and his horse inside the pen with us. He had also built a nice loop and was already making his way down toward the day's troublemaker.

Dwight and I had been working horses and cattle together for years, and it wasn't uncommon for us to go through an entire day of branding or sorting or doctoring without saying more than a few words. Not because we didn't like one another, but rather because there was usually no need to talk. We both knew what job needed to get done, and we just did it. When we did communicate, it was often with a nod or other gesture, or sometimes a word or two.

In this situation, we both knew what needed to be done: get the gelding under control and the mare and baby out of the pen, into the trailer, and on their way to the ranch. Why this gelding seemed to be so infatuated with the baby didn't matter. The job needed to be done, and that was that.

Dwight trotted his horse to about the middle of the hundred- by forty-foot pen, then eased the horse into a walk as he moved closer to the gelding, who by now seemed to have all of his attention back on the mare and baby at the other end. The horse didn't even seem to know Dwight was there, although I'm sure he did. Dwight began to ease his loop into an arc over his head as he closed in on the gelding, but before he got close enough to do anything with it, the big red horse suddenly bolted back toward the mare and baby.

Dwight expertly tossed his loop as the gelding passed him, and from my perspective, it looked like he was going to catch him easily. But then, just as the loop was about to drop down over the gelding's head, he ever so slightly dipped that big ol' Roman nose of his, causing the rope to skip harmlessly off his ears, bounce off his rump, and miss him completely. As he galloped straight for the mare, Buck and I were all that stood in his way.

In the time it took me to glance around and check on where the mare and baby were and turn back, he had pretty effectively covered the length of the pen and was almost right on top of us. I had a good loop built, but little time to do anything with it other than toss it out in front of him and hope I caught something. Dwight would later tell me it was the ugliest job of rope-throwing he'd ever seen, and by the way it felt as it left my hand, I'm sure he was right. Yet, somehow, that awkwardly thrown loop found its way over the big gelding's head, dropping down around his neck and allowing me to take up the slack and slow him down.

It was clear almost as soon as the loop slipped around his neck that this was not the first time he'd been roped. Instead of panicking or fighting the rope once he felt it tighten, like most horses would in the same situation, he gave in to it immediately. As Buck and I loped along with him, it was fairly easy to get him turned away from the mare and baby.

Within seconds, however, he gave a sharp pull and tried to turn back toward them. I took a quick dally, which all but stopped him in his tracks, then Dwight came loping up and moved in from behind, pushing him away from his targets. With me on the rope and Dwight pushing from behind, we were able to get the gelding across the pen, where I looped my rope around one of the heavy wooden fence posts. I was a little surprised to see that he stood pretty well once he was secured, and other than some frantic ground-pawing and screaming at the top of his lungs, he caused no more trouble from that point forward.

Dwight and I finally dismounted, and he took our horses back to the trailer. I retrieved the halter I had dropped in the dirt when the gelding jumped the gate, and Dwight brought an extra halter back with him from the truck. He eased up to the mare, slipped it over her nose, and buckled it into place. I took the other halter, and removing the lead rope, turned it upside down and slid it over the exhausted baby's head. By turning it upside down, the part of the halter that would normally be over an average-sized horse's nose was down around the base of the baby's neck, and the strap that would normally go behind an adult horse's ears and over the poll was now around the baby's girth area. By buckling that strap into place around the girth, the halter effectively became a small harness, something like folks use when walking their dogs.

It was the first chance we had to see the baby up close. He was a handsome fellow, dark brown like his mother, with a dished face; big, inquisitive eyes; and straight legs. Unfortunately, he also had cuts on his chest and front legs from what looked like being run into or through a barbed wire fence, and he had a number of bite marks on his neck, back, flanks, and hindquarters.

With Dwight leading the mare and me using the halter/harness to guide the baby, we took them to the trailer and got them loaded. Our saddle horses were in the nose of the stock trailer, the middle compartment was empty, and the mare and baby were in the back compartment. We then hauled the trailer a good quarter-mile away before going back to turn the big gelding loose.

Things were quiet in the truck as we headed back to the ranch—not unusual after a long day. The quiet allowed my mind time to drift back to what I had seen the mare do that afternoon in simultaneously defending her baby from the gelding and guiding the baby away from him. I played the scene over and over in my head: the power of the kick that came from the back end of the mare, the total softness coming from the front. I was amazed at how quickly the foal moved with just that soft touch from his mother, particularly considering how tired he was at the time.

I began to wonder if there might be a way for humans to harness, or replicate, the type of powerful softness the mare had displayed. The problem was, at the time, I had never heard anybody talk about it or seen anybody doing anything like it. In fact, as I gave it more thought, I began to realize that the two words didn't even seem to fit together: powerful softness. Was it an oxymoron? Was it something only animals possessed? Did it even exist, or was I just imagining it? Could it be, or was it already being, developed and used in some form in the human world?

My thoughts shifted to the foal riding in the back of the trailer. I wondered if he had nursed at all during the day. I wondered where I was going to put him and his mom once we got back to the ranch. I'd heard the weather was going to turn bad in the next couple of days and wondered if he'd be strong enough by then to make it through the kind of spring storms that are common in the mountains. About that time, Dwight cleared his throat, the way he always did just before he got ready to say something.

"People pay a lot of money for horses that can jump that high," he said, interrupting my train of thought.

"What?"

"I was just sayin' you could probably make a jumping horse out of that gelding."

"Not much call for jumping horses in the dude business."

"Yeah, I suppose not." He turned his attention out the window of the truck. "Still, he sure jumps good." He paused for a couple of seconds. A herd of Black Angus cattle milled around in a large open field, and a handful of three-day-old calves took off running and bucking, tails high and heads swinging. He smiled. "I sure like this time of year."

I watched the calves as they began to playfully butt heads, their mothers grazing peacefully nearby.

"Me too," I said.

Softness from the Inside Out

Angela Ewing

Just months ago, I was coming home from work physically exhausted, with pain burning in my shoulders, lower back, and hip joints. I recall those first few moments when, retiring for the night, my body seemed to find relief. My job as a Physician Assistant, which I consider a life's reward to be able to do, requires a commitment of time as well as physical sacrifice.

Our bodies are amazing in their ability to respond to what we require. In my case, that involves standing for sometimes six hours in one position, keeping my hands within a narrow range (approximately mid-chest to waist level), focusing intently through a microscope. Frequently, I am required to wear a heavy lead vest and skirt for the majority of the day.

It took my work in improving my relationship and connection with my horse to make me realize that my job was affecting my posture, the way I stood, walked, sat, and most importantly, the way I was riding my horse.

Over the last thirteen years, I had begun resting all of my weight on my right leg and hip, unaware that I was intermittently locking my knees, hollowing my lower back, and standing off-center. I had found a way to "rest" my body as it tired from long hours of standing. In one of Mark's clinics, we unfolded the layers of physical hindrance of my presentation to my horse. It became obvious in the way my horse moved that the problems began with me. It showed in my inability to round and soften my back, which came from the overdevelopment of opposing muscles that I had built while "managing" a position at work. During a lesson with Mark, I was able to find my center, which affected my balance and immediately changed my horse's movement. It was a light-bulb moment for me to realize that for all the work I had been doing to connect with my horse, I had not completely connected to myself. I had pieces of the puzzle, but not all of them.

I have spent the last few months retraining my body to maintain the correct position all the time. Standing in line at the grocery store, driving my car, walking, and—where I spend most of my time—at work. It has been an amazing experience to find a way to consciously soften myself from inside out. My back and hips no longer hurt. I have muscles in my shoulders that I never knew existed. The ones that were in constant spasm are now relaxed. When I have to retract an incision with an instrument, I find I no longer use muscle, no matter how long I am required to do so. I use my core and the energy from within to complete the task. Most importantly, I breathe—the deep kind of breathing, which is where you find your center. My hope is that, over time, I won't have to think about it so much; it will become second nature.

It never ceases to amaze me how horses continue to teach us more about the human experience just by their presence in our lives. It requires a conscious effort on my part to offer my horse presence of moment, and I must remember to do the same for myself. In doing so, I learn to do something that ultimately affects everything . . . including my horse.

The Pull 2

While seeing the mare with her baby may have been the first time I became consciously aware of the idea of powerful softness, it was not my first introduction to the overall concept of softness when it came to horses. The old horseman I worked with when I was a kid—whom I've always called the Old Man—had introduced me to it years before. Of course, I don't recall him using the word softness much, if at all. Back then, instead of telling me when something was soft, he would simply point out when it wasn't.

When I was about eleven, I was riding a little gelding named Spark and was having trouble getting him to turn and stop. If I pulled to the right, he would pull to the left; if I pulled to the left, he would pull to the right. If I pulled on him to try to get a stop, he would push into my hands and just keep walking forward. The longer I rode him, the more frustrated I got, and the more he seemed to want to fight with me.

Keep in mind that regardless of age, both humans and horses work to the level of their knowledge base and life experience. This was certainly true in my case while I was working with Spark. At the time, I hadn't ridden very many horses, so my knowledge base was limited to things that I had ridden, such as a bicycle. With a bicycle, when you turn the handlebars to the left, the thing goes to the left. When you turn them to the right, it goes to the right. When you stop pedaling, it stops. I guess I just naturally assumed that a horse would operate the same way.

It's the way an eleven-year-old thinks. Until he knows better, a horse and a bicycle are basically the same thing to him. Intellectually, there is a gap that keeps him from understanding that a bicycle is a machine that always does what it is told, when it is told, and horse is a living, breathing, thinking animal with ideas, feelings, and emotions. In the child's mind, both things should operate basically the same way. That is why a child with a limited knowledge base will become frustrated pretty quickly when a horse expresses its feelings, ideas, and emotions while being ridden.

At any rate, the Old Man had been watching me for a while as I struggled to do just about anything with Spark. Then I guess he just couldn't stand it anymore, and finally walked up to us. The gelding and I had just finished a monumental battle, which started out in the front pasture. After all my efforts to get Spark to turn one way, then the other, and finally to stop had failed, he dragged the two of us unceremoniously over to the hay barn, where Spark put his nose on the faded-yellow brick wall and just stood there.

"Horses don't like to be pulled on," the Old Man said drily, petting Spark on the neck.

"I wasn't pulling on him, he was pulling on me!" I argued as only an eleven-year-old could. "Every time I try to make him do anything, he just wants to do something else. He doesn't want to turn, he doesn't want to stop, he doesn't want to . . ."

The Old Man held up his well-weathered, calloused hand, signaling me to stop talking, which I did. Even at eleven, I knew better than to talk into a hand that looked like that. He reached down, and with two fingers, picked up the left rein, the one closest to him. Then, lifting the rein and using hardly any effort, he easily turned Spark's head toward him. He gently lowered the rein, then reached across Spark's neck and took hold of the right rein. He repeated the same action, and Spark responded by effortlessly turning his head to the right. He lowered the rein, allowing Spark's head to straighten. Then, while still holding the right rein, he took hold of the left rein with his left hand and again, with gentle and minimal contact on both reins, he induced Spark to willingly back up.

He backed Spark seven or eight feet away from the wall, then let go of the right rein. Still holding the left rein, he led the two of us back out into the pasture where all the trouble had begun.

"Horses don't like to be pulled on," he repeated. Then he turned Spark and me loose and walked away.

Though I had no way of knowing at the time, what I had just witnessed was an expertly performed demonstration of softness, through what many in the horse world these days might refer to as "feel." Of course, both concepts completely escaped me at the time. On that day, my understanding of what I had seen was that he just hadn't pulled as hard as I did, and somehow, the gelding responded. So I replicated what I thought I saw the Old Man do, and in return, I started getting better responses from Spark. Not responses as good as the Old Man's, mind you, but better than before he stepped in.

Like a lot of people, I suppose, I had a very difficult time understanding the concept of how not to pull. After all, it is in most animals' nature, including humans, to pull back when being pulled on, and to push back against something that is pushing them. And of course, the more one has been pushed or pulled, the more defensive one will have a tendency to become. For instance, a horse whose mouth has been consistently pulled will often get to the point that when a rider makes any contact with the reins whatsoever, it will automatically go on the defensive and lean into the pressure. This, in turn, often causes the rider to pull on the reins, which just perpetuates the cycle.

Breaking such a cycle isn't always easy, especially when you don't know what else to do. Yet it was the Old Man and his simple observation that really helped get me thinking differently.

A few weeks after my initial struggle with Spark, he and I were out in the pasture trying again. Things were not going well. I could see the Old Man watching us from the door of the tack room as Spark swung one way, then the other, then back again, always in a direction opposite of where I wanted him to go. He shook his head, pawed at the ground, swished his tail, kicked out with his back feet, and snorted hard through his nose. Undeterred, I still tried to get his head around in a turn, so much so that at one point, I was actually pulling one rein with both hands, trying to get him to come around to the right. And we were still going to the left!

Again, I think the Old Man stayed quiet about as long as he could before he finally made his way out to the pasture where Spark and I continued to whirl around. As he got up next to us, the Old Man reached out and took hold of the rein I was pulling on. Almost as soon as he touched the rein, two things happened. The first was that I no longer wanted to pull on the rein. It was as though his grasp took all my strength away, and my entire body, which just a second before had been as tight as Dick's hatband, immediately began to relax. The second thing was that Spark stopped moving, and after standing there for a couple of seconds, lowered his head and relaxed.

It was the first time I had ever felt anything like that. Through his touch on the rein, the Old Man had somehow established a connection between the three of us that completely dispersed our tension and replaced it with a sort of softness. It was an amazing feeling, one that I would not have again for a very long time.

"Things would work a lot better with this gelding," he quietly said, "if you'd stop pulling on him."

"I don't know how to do that," I said in frustration.

"How to do what?"

"Not pull!"

The Old Man, still holding the rein, stood quietly for a few seconds, his face like stone. Then, ever so slowly, a slight smile moved across his face, as if he realized how difficult it would be to picture yourself not doing something. He nodded as if agreeing with me.

"Why don't you put him up for now?" It was more of a suggestion than a statement. "We'll try again tomorrow."

As I looked down at the rare smile in the Old Man's eyes, my frustration slowly began to wane. I placed the rein I was holding down on Spark's neck.

"Okay," I said as I climbed down. The three of us then turned and walked up to the barn.

It was toward the end of the day, and after putting Spark up and finishing a few chores, I took my bike from where I had leaned it against the side of the barn and pushed it around front. Just as I threw a leg over and was getting ready to start pedaling down the driveway, the Old Man came out of the tack room door, an ever-present cigarette between his fingers.

"Bye," I chirped, the frustration of earlier in the afternoon already a distant memory.

"Hold on." He stepped out of the tack room and walked over to where I was sitting on my bike. He looked down at my hands on the handlebars, took a drag from his cigarette, and blew a stream of bluish smoke from the corner of his mouth. "Go ahead and ride your bike around in a little circle here." He pointed at the dirt-covered yard we were standing in and drew a circle in the air.

I did what he asked without bothering to ask why. He watched me ride the circle a couple of times, then pointed again and drew a circle in the air in the opposite direction.

"Now the other way," he said, taking another drag on his cigarette.

I briefly stopped pedaling and effortlessly coasted into a nice little half-circle that looped me back in the other direction. I began pedaling again. I made about two more circles before he drew another circle in the air, indicating he wanted me to go back the other way, which I did. After two more circles, he motioned for me to stop.

"The way you steer your bike," he said, mashing out the cigarette butt on the heel of his boot, "that's how you ride a horse without pulling on 'im." He then field-dressed the now-extinguished cigarette, tobacco drifting toward the ground as he pinched and rolled the remainder of the paper between his fingers, and walked past me back into the tack room. "See you tomorrow," he said as he disappeared through the wooden door.

I waited for just a second to see if he might come back out, and then turned my bike toward the quarter-mile-long driveway, pushed myself into motion, and pedaled for the front gate. There weren't any horses in the front pasture, so the front gate was open. I breezed past it and onto the gravel road, standing on the pedals as I pumped hard to gain speed. As soon as I was moving at an acceptable velocity, I began my daily ritual of swerving in a big serpentine line from one bar ditch, across the road to the bar ditch on the opposite side, then back again. I repeated the pattern all the way to where the pavement started, a distance of about a half-mile. Very few cars traveled the gravel part of that road, and I always enjoyed the opportunity to use as much of it as I wanted.

The Old Man's comparison between steering my bike and turning a horse without pulling meant little to me when he said it. But as I swerved my bike from the edge of one ditch to the other, I slowly became aware of what it actually took to steer my little Schwinn Stingray. I noticed that turning to the right, for instance, I used just slightly more draw with my right hand than push with my left. The same went for a left-hand turn. In fact, regardless of direction, both hands felt as though they had very close to an equal amount of contact as I moved from one turn to the next.

The more I paid attention, the more I noticed I was barely even holding the grips as I eased the handlebars in one direction or the other. With such a negligible grip on the bars, it was sometimes difficult to know if I was pushing or pulling the bike into a turn. As I reached the pavement, I straightened the bike out and took it to the right side of the road, where I stayed as I pedaled the rest of the way home.

Admittedly, as I reached the pavement that day, I lost track of the feel between the handlebars and my hands. My mind was on to other, more important eleven-year-old-boy things, such as trying to decide what position I would have later that evening when some of us boys from the neighborhood played baseball.

Of course, I had no way of knowing at the time that what I had felt during that ride was at the heart of the very kind of softness that not only created those smooth turns with my bike but can also create positive responses in horses, people, dogs, cats, and myriad other animals, not to mention some machines and even inanimate objects (we'll talk more about that later).

It's funny, but I couldn't even begin to count how many times that particular day has popped into my consciousness. I suppose that's because I have given a great deal of thought to the concept of softness over the years, and in doing so, have come to realize that softness begins (and I emphasize the word begins) with one simple truth: It's not what we do that starts us on the path to softness, but rather, it's what we don't do. When talking specifically about working with horses, it is my belief that softness begins with learning how not to pull or push. In other words, we find a way to take the adversarial emotion out of a situation that pulling and pushing creates, and replace it with one of neutrality.

Now, I suppose some folks might look at that last statement and say to themselves, Hey, wait a minute . . . I don't use adversarial emotion when I'm with my horse. The truth is, very few conscientious horse people would ever intentionally go into a situation with an adversarial mindset (although there are certainly those who do). Mostly what I'm talking about here is how easy it is to turn a relatively innocuous exchange with a horse into a battle simply by the way we use our hands on the reins, no matter how mindful we are.

Here's an example. Let's say that a rider asks the horse to turn to the right. (We are assuming that the horse is relatively well trained and is fitted with a snaffle bit, or any similar rig that works off direct pressure.) The rider takes a little contact with the right rein, asking the horse to follow a "soft feel" (which we will discuss later) so that the horse turns right. The horse begins to turn, but then for whatever reason, stops following that feel, or worse, offers to go back to the left. The rider, feeling a resistance in the rein, begins to apply more pressure to get the horse to continue to the right. However, within that pressure, the rider is almost always adding a pull to one degree or another, and it is that pull that gets in the way of the sensitivity we need in order to feel when and if the horse tries to "give." When the horse ultimately tries to give to the pressure, the rider inadvertently takes what the horse is giving. The horse, not feeling a release from the pressure (pull) that the rider is applying, feels he is doing the wrong thing by trying to give. As a result, he puts more pressure back in the opposite direction, and just like that, an adversarial situation is born.

No such intent on the rider's part was present during the entire encounter, but it still didn't change the feel of the situation. As far as the horse is concerned, if the rider is going to pull, the horse is going to defend himself by pulling back. So even though the rider may not be looking at the situation in an adversarial way, the horse may be. And when the horse defends himself, the rider is ultimately going to do the same. Pretty quickly, we have two individuals pulling on one another, with the rider wondering why the horse is fighting the turn!

I think it's important to understand that most animals, humans and horses included, will (at least initially) fight resistance in an attempt to physically overpower it. Or, if unable to overpower the resistance, they either give into it or search for some other non-confrontational way around it.

An example that most horse folks have probably seen at one time or another is when a horse becomes frightened and suddenly sets back against something it's tied to. Assuming that nothing breaks, such as the halter, lead rope, hitch rail, post, or whatever, it is typical to see the horse pull, flail, shake its head violently from side to side, and lean backward with all its weight. Then, when the horse finds that none of that behavior actually relieves the physical pressure it's experiencing, it will simply jump forward. In doing so, it is finally able to relieve the pressure.

At its core, this scenario is a great example of the idea of "not pulling." Sure, the horse in this situation is pulling. However, the post or hitch rail it's tied to is not. And it is this concept that I believe the Old Man was trying to get across to me all those years ago.

You see, the horse in this situation may be pulling against the post or hitch rail, but the post or hitch rail is neutral—a solid entity that is just there and not fighting against the horse's pull. Because the post or hitch rail is not actively pulling back or working against the horse's resistance, the horse usually figures out fairly quickly that it is only fighting itself. Often, a horse in this situation will realize that if it relaxes just a bit or moves even the slightest bit toward the post or hitch rail, it will immediately get relief from its situation.

Several years ago, I gave this idea of "not pulling" serious thought, and decided to see just how much or how little one would need to do to get a release while pulling against something that wasn't pulling back. I used this particular scenario of a horse setting back against a hitch rail as my test situation.

The experiment was fairly simple and straightforward. I looped a lead rope over a very stout hitch rail, then, holding the other end of the rope, I leaned back on the rope and against the hitch rail using all my weight and strength. Two things became immediately apparent. The first was that if I relaxed any part of my body, even a little, as I pulled, I felt an immediate overall relaxation in the rest of my body, which made it difficult to continue to pull at the same level of intensity. The second was that if I moved even the slightest amount, and I mean the slightest amount, in the direction of the hitch rail, I received an exponentially significant release in the amount of tension I felt between the hitch rail and myself. In fact, if I moved the hand in which I held the lead rope even one-sixteenth of an inch toward the hitch rail, a considerable amount of slack would immediately develop in the rope—again, making it nearly impossible for me to continue to pull.

This little experiment really got me to think about how little we, as riders, have to do in order to help horses find a release, and how little horses have to do to get one—assuming, of course, that we aren't pulling on them in the first place.

However, even though I'm discussing the concept of "not pulling" here and using the example of a solid barrier such as a hitch rail or post to do so, I am certainly not advocating that we try to be as rigid as posts when we ride. Actually, I am advocating quite the opposite. The more fluid we are in our movements when we ride, the more fluidity in movement the horse will ultimately be able to achieve. And herein lies the paradox of horsemanship.

Many folks ride with tremendous stiffness and use pulling as the main way to direct and/or communicate with the horse through the reins. What is really needed is to ride with suppleness and fluidity, and to develop the art of not pulling while still being firm enough with our hands to allow the horse to find the correct answers to the requests we transmit through the reins.

It should be noted that the kind of stiffness and pulling I've been talking about is not limited to our work in the saddle. Many folks inadvertently use the same type of negative resistance (increasing intensity to an already averse situation) when they work with their horses on the ground as well. An example of this might be what often happens when folks try to load a horse in a trailer.

Many horse owners will load their horses by entering the trailer in front of the horse, then "pulling" on the lead rope to encourage the horse to get in. A horse in this situation will often offer some forward movement, but again, because the owner is tense and pulling, he or she is unable to feel the horse's try. So, when the horse offers the forward movement, the owner inadvertently continues to pull, which in turn causes the horse to pull against the owner's pull. Often, this results in the horse backing a substantial distance from the trailer, dragging the owner (who by now is hanging on to the rope for dear life) with it. In cases where the horse was, say, half-way in the trailer when the owner started to pull, the resistance that the owner puts on the rope usually results in the horse pulling back so hard it ends up whacking its head on the ceiling of the trailer. Many a vet has been called out to put stitches in a horse that's injured its head in such a way.

Along these same lines, there are also situations where a horse might go into the trailer just fine, and even travel without incident. But then, upon reaching the destination, it refuses to back out of the trailer. In this situation, the handler might resort to getting in the trailer with the horse and trying to push the animal out, either by using backward force on the lead rope or pushing on the horse's head or chest. Of course, this usually causes the horse to push into the handler, which causes the handler to push harder, which causes the horse to push harder and . . . well, I think you get the idea.

Looking back, I believe the Old Man had tried, the best way he knew how, to help me understand that these types of pulling and pushing matches between horse and human simply aren't necessary, and they most certainly aren't effective. In fact, it is the pushing and pulling that not only gets in the way of developing softness in the horse, but can also make it almost impossible for the human to develop softness as well. As a result, I believe that before we can even begin to work toward developing softness in either horse or human, we must first try to understand and eliminate, or at least limit, those things that inherently cause us to go in completely the opposite direction. Pushing and pulling are at the top of that list.

For many of us, eliminating that push/pull within ourselves can be difficult. During times like these, there is often a breakdown in awareness and sensitivity that simply doesn't allow us to recognize that we are using negative resistance in the first place. I believe the reason for this is that we sometimes get so focused on the problem that we find it difficult to see, or even know, that a solution is available to us. The solution can be both physically and emotionally counterintuitive, not only affecting the way we ride and handle our horses, but also the way we live our everyday lives. Many of us practice (albeit usually inadvertently) resistance in other aspects in our life, then bring that resistance to our horses when we ride or work with them.

Now, I would imagine at least some folks just read that last statement and are saying to themselves: I don't practice resistance!

Well, the truth is, we all practice resistance in some form or another on a daily basis. We just aren't aware of it. The bottom line? Whenever we use more effort or muscle than is needed to do something simple, like picking up a glass or a cup of coffee, or pulling on our boots or closing a door, or sitting down in a chair or picking up a fork or spoon, we are practicing resistance.

Regardless of the task, if we use more effort than is actually needed, we are, by definition, engaging more muscle than the situation requires. As a result, not only do our own muscles work against each other, creating resistance in our body, but also, we ultimately dull our sensitivities. So we don't notice the texture of the Styrofoam cup our coffee is in, or the texture and thickness of the leather our boots are made from as we pull them on our feet. We don't recognize the strengths, or possibly the weaknesses, in the construction of the chair we are sitting in, or the weight of the door as we swing it closed, or the temperature our metal spoon or fork transmits.

It is my belief that becoming aware of how we participate in the world on a daily basis and how we perform our everyday, mundane, or not-so-mundane tasks adds to our ability, or inability, to develop the kind of awareness and sensitivity it takes to be really good at working with horses. Developing the kind of awareness and "feel" it takes to realize when we are working against our horse doesn't begin with working with our horse. It begins by doing all of those everyday things with as much feel and awareness as we possibly can, and then bringing that awareness to our horse.

All those years ago, when the Old Man had me take a look at how I was steering my bicycle, what he was really showing me was how to become aware. He was showing me that I was already directing my bike through softness and feel, not forcing it with strength and muscle as I had been when I was working with Spark. He was showing me that what I needed to do to work with Spark successfully, I was already doing in at least one other aspect of my life. I just didn't know it at the time.

It would take years for me to understand the brilliance and simplicity of what he tried to share with me that day. It would take me even longer to find ways to implement it.

Offering the Inside of Ourselves to Our Horses

Shannon Brown

When Mark asked if I could share my thoughts on softness, feel, and connection, I must admit I had to think for quite some time about how I could answer what those three words mean to me in my horsemanship and my life. The only word I could come up with was everything. Softness, feel, and connection mean everything to me.

Obviously, just writing that one word wouldn't make for much of a story, so I had to think about the question a little more. I realized that it was during the moments where softness, feel, and connection were the most out of balance or lacking in my life that I had learned the most about myself and my horsemanship.

I have worked with Mark for almost a decade, both as a student and as a student instructor, and I have to admit, before meeting Mark, I didn't put much thought into these three attributes. I knew I was missing something, but didn't know what. I had ridden since I was three, and I imagine that, to a certain degree, those three attributes existed in my horsemanship, but not to the level I needed, and certainly not to the degree required to work with troubled horses. As I sorted through almost ten years of memories and the horses I have sought help with, both my own and those I had in training, a common thread surfaced: when I lost the internal connection with myself, I wasn't operating with much softness or feel. When I strayed from working on myself and started working on the horses, as many of us do, I got further and further from the kind of work I was trying to do. I was just working on the surface, on the outside.

While I have many positive moments to reflect on, times I can say that I felt I was achieving some level of softness, feel, and connection in my work, I have more of the moments during which I was operating with very few of these concepts. It was in those moments of trying to find balance and offer the horse something worthwhile that I realized what I was missing: internal softness and connection. This is not something you try on for size; it is who you become, who you are on the inside. It is not something you do—rather, it is who you are.

In late summer 2008, my husband left for a yearlong tour of duty in Iraq as an infantry company commander. Having been in the army myself for almost eight years, I thought this wouldn't be too difficult for me to handle, as we had coped with deployments before. His deployment not only left me to care for our home and run my horse-training business alone, but also to act as a mentor to an entire company of spouses and their children while their husbands were similarly deployed.

I am not one to necessarily know when I have too much on my proverbial plate, so I was training four to seven horses full time as well as traveling in Colorado and to California to teach. I thought this was a great idea, as it would keep me busy while my husband was gone. As life sometimes shows us, things were going well right up until the moment something changed, and there was no way to see that something coming.

After a long day of working with the horses, I was making dinner when the phone rang. The voice on the other end took my breath away and sent chills up my spine. There had been a suicide-bomber attack on my husband's company, and several soldiers had been killed. A communication blackout followed, which made it impossible to find out any further details; I had no idea if my husband was safe. Time stood still. Seconds felt like minutes and minutes felt like hours. I realized that life had just gotten very real. I also realized how very alone I felt out there on our little six-and-a-half-acre ranch in rural Colorado. I didn't have a plan for something like this. For the first time in a long time, I had no idea what to do in the next moment. I was frozen.

In the days and weeks that followed, I discovered that my husband was safe, but I also discovered that one of my dearest friends had just lost her husband; he was one of six soldiers who had died in the attack. I can honestly tell you, this is one of those life moments where you just wish there was an instruction booklet so you knew what to do. As I began supporting the family members and attending funeral services for the men we had lost,

I was both honored and humbled to be part of something so utterly life-changing. In one breath, there was complete devastation and in another, there was seeing Americans and their small towns at their finest as they honored our fallen soldiers. I was forever changed by the experience.

In the months that followed, I continued to forge on and work my business. At the time, I didn't see any other way. I had a job to do, and I was also trying to keep myself busy so I didn't have to deal with the fear and grief that crept in with the realities of combat. Looking back, it's clear I was heading for a disaster . . . or two. As I motored on, almost completely checked out with myself, accidents started to happen. First I came off a horse, hard, and hit my head. At the time, I was convinced it came out of nowhere. Then I stepped off another horse that was just in for a "tune up" and got my foot hung up in the stirrup. She bolted sideways and I found myself being dragged across my arena. Luckily, I was able to kick free before too much damage was done. As I lay there watching the mare run laps around me, I remember thinking, What the hell is happening? I am working so hard and getting my butt kicked. I never come off horses, and I don't need this right now. This year has been hard enough.

After I lay there for what seemed like an eternity, emotions started to well up. I couldn't deal with what was surfacing, so I shoved it back down, dusted myself off, and went back to work. Being strong for others made it hard for me to fall apart. In fact, I was afraid to fall apart. I can only imagine what it felt like to be in my presence, especially for an animal as sensitive and present as the horse.

Everyone who works with horses for a living has that one horse—more, if we are lucky—that teaches you more about yourself in a short period of time than you could learn in ten or fifteen years. Mine was a little black mare that came in from the Midwest for training. Scarcely fourteen hands, she stepped off the trailer and was quiet. Too quiet. As I led her down to her paddock, I noticed that she didn't seem to be on the other end of the lead rope, and not in a good way. I turned her loose to stretch her legs after the long trailer ride. As it turns out, that was the last time I got a halter on or off her for almost two weeks. She woke up twenty-four hours after arriving, bouncing off the walls of her paddock, terrified. I remembered Mark talking about his work with mustangs and how all he could offer them at times was consistency.

I decided to be that consistent person coming in and out of her pen bringing her food and water for as long as it took. For several days, this is all I did for the little mare. At first, even that was too much for her, and she stayed at the back of her pen, watching my every move. As the days passed, she was able to come a little closer with each feeding. After about two weeks, she let my hand graze her neck after dropping her hay in her paddock, and she didn't bolt or brace her body. I couldn't believe how much humans troubled this little mare. I also couldn't see any parallels between her inner storm and my own. After a couple of weeks, we had progressed to touching, grooming, haltering, and leading in the paddock, so I thought it was as good a day as any to lead her around the barnyard.

Once we stepped through the barn doors, she bolted—ripped the rope out of my hands and tore off up the driveway. Boy, that was discouraging. This behavior, as well as rearing while I tried to get her ready to be turned loose on pasture, went on for a week or two. Eventually, I was able to get some sort of feel on the end of a lead rope. While she was doing better, I could still feel a level of fear and self-preservation; she was not soft. Looking back, neither was I.

The mare and I continued to work together, and after a couple of more weeks, she was wearing her saddle, working in the round pen, leading and tying and loading in the trailer with a decent feel. I thought we were doing pretty well, considering where we had started, but there was still something missing; I knew I wasn't going to be getting on her anytime soon.

I was due to link up with Mark for a clinic at a mutual friend's house in Colorado and help out with the students. I decided to bring the mare so she could go for a trailer ride and spend a few days in another location. In my spare time, I would work with her. I also wanted to ask Mark for a little help. I am pretty careful about asking for help after long clinic sessions, as I realize that after putting in eight to ten hours a day teaching, we are both pretty tired. But if there was ever a horse I wanted some advice on, she was it. After the third day of teaching, Mark decided to take a look and see how he could help me with the mare. As we walked to her paddock at dusk, I began explaining what I had been working on with her, and how things had been going between us.

"She sometimes bolts out of nowhere and rips right out of my hands while I am leading her," I explained as I slipped her halter on, not even aware that the mare had not bolted for at least two weeks.

"You might want to soften your hand," Mark said quietly, as we walked side by side toward the indoor arena.

"What do you mean?" I asked.

"Soften your hand. Open your hand on the lead rope. You are holding on so tightly that you are telling her she should be ready to bolt," he said casually.

"Oh," I said sheepishly, as I became aware that not only my hand was tight, but my entire body was tight. The last thing I wanted to have happen was to have this mare rip out of my hands and go running all over the property after a long day of teaching. Well, she didn't. She was walking quietly behind me, as though she had lived on the property all her life.

"Why don't you show me what you have been working on with her, and I will see where I can help you out," he said, as he took a seat near the gate of the indoor arena. As I began working with the mare on a lunge line, I realized how rarely I had Mark's undivided attention at the end of a long day of work, and was very grateful for the opportunity to get some much-needed help now.

She began buzzing around on the lunge line, looking panicked.

"So is this how things have been going?" Mark asked as the mare zipped past him in a streak of black.

"Mostly, yes. While she's gotten better, she still seems so afraid much of the time."

"So, what exactly are you looking for here?" Mark asked.

I had worked with Mark long enough to know that this question is really not a question at all. Rather, it's a question I had heard before when it was clear to him that I didn't really know what I was looking for, which—though not obvious to me—was very apparent to Mark and the horse.

"Well, I am looking for some sort of connection with her, rather than her just buzzing around on the end of the lead in a panic," I answered, as though it should be obvious.

"You've done some really good work here getting her through some rough spots, but there is something missing for both of you. Do you mind if I take her for a few minutes?" he asked as he slowly stood up.

As I handed the rope to Mark, I noticed that the mare locked onto his center and quieted immediately. As he stepped to the right, she tracked his movement. Then he stepped to the left, and she continued to track him. She seemed to be glued to something inside him. At a moment like this, I know better than to verbalize this thought, but I wanted to say was, What the hell did you just do? As I watched them work together, it was clear that he was offering the mare something that I was not. It was instant and amazing to watch, and I was very aware in that moment that she had been asking for something from me for a while, and I had not been offering it. I felt an underlying emotion start to well up, one that I had been holding onto so tightly for several months. Great, just what I want to do right now is fall apart, I thought, trying to get myself under control.

Mark obviously sensed the change, because what he said next caused the tears to slowly spill over.

"You know, sometimes we just have to allow ourselves to fall apart rather than keep holding on to something and trying to be okay." He'd only had the mare for a few minutes, but that was all it took for me to see what was missing. "You aren't very connected to yourself right now, and yet you are asking her to connect to you. If you could connect to yourself and show her that you are the safe place for her to be, then she might feel a little better about connecting with you."

As I took the lead rope, the feel was so different that tears continued to fall slowly. It amazed me to find that as I allowed myself to let go of my stored emotions, the little mare was able to let go of her own. Together, tension melted away and we were able to work on connection, softness, and feel. Finally, the many hours spent with her showed up, and she felt better about life than I thought she could. So did I. It was a profound moment in my horsemanship. In those moments, I felt a level of connection that I don't think I had ever accessed with a horse, and it came from the horse I would have least expected. Suddenly, I could see things so clearly. I had stopped working on what was going on inside of me because that was too painful, and tried to work on the horses and what was going on inside of them. There was nothing wrong with what the horses had going on inside of them.

In the end, it really isn't about working on the horse. It is about what level we are willing to work on the inside of ourselves, and in turn, offer the horse. Those places are easier to access some times than others, but I believe we can get there if we look deeply enough and are willing to get up the next day and try again. Once you find that level of internal connection, you know, and it's a feeling you want to experience over and over again. You also certainly know when you start to lose it. It becomes a relationship, both with yourself and with the horse. As one of my favorite musicians David Wilcox says, "When you're working on a relationship, that's the only way we get our own selves tuned up. Figure out how to be who we need to be. It's a lot of work, but it's good work . . . if you can get it."

It's that feeling with horses that keeps me coming back for more time after time, and I am grateful I have had a mentor to help me along my horsemanship journey.

Internal 3
Softness

Over the years, I have come to understand that one of the keys to developing true softness in oneself is by practicing it full time. It is not a skill that can be mastered with part-time application. For instance, I believe it is very difficult for people to become skillful at being soft if they only practice it while working with their horses. Sure, that would be a good start, and ideally, if one became soft with a horse, eventually that softness would begin to permeate other aspects of life. But the truth is, unless softness is a way of life, it is extremely difficult to master.

If a person were only trying to be soft with a horse but not when driving a car; setting down a glass; shoveling manure; sitting in a chair; talking with co-workers, strangers, friends, or family members; or during any number of other daily activities, it seems to me that the art is not being practiced in an overall mindful way. For those folks, softness is something they do but not who they are. For me, there is a big difference between the two.

For a very long time, I thought I understood what true softness was. In fact, I felt I was fairly accomplished at being able to develop softness when working with horses, and even in other aspects of my life. Back then, I, like so many others who work with horses, made the assumption that somehow softness came from the hands, and if I could just get my hands soft enough, my horses would become soft as well.

Don't get me wrong—that way of thinking served me well for a very long time. Overall, the horses I worked with would become soft in the bridle and soft in the body. But still, I always felt like something was missing, or maybe a better way to say it is that I felt I was missing something.

Still, the truth is, I can't really point to any one situation, horse, or event that stopped me in my tracks and started me on the path of looking deeper into the subject. Rather, things just sort of shifted for me over time. Instead of looking to horse professionals, horse books, and magazine articles to help me improve my skills, I found I was slowly being drawn to other, seemingly unrelated subjects, such as martial arts, Eastern history and philosophy, and even certain occupational and physical therapies, as well as particular pieces of music and certain musicians.

Around that time, I began to closely observe some of the masters in the martial arts world, particularly those in aikido, an art I had been studying and training in for several years. I started seeing a number of similarities in those old masters' movement and techniques. Primarily, I began to notice the seemingly effortless way the masters were able to not only move their own bodies, but also the bodies of their training partners. While this effortlessness of movement was impressive, the power that was being generated by these individuals during their movements was even more impressive. It was a power of mind and body I found to be very similar to that exhibited by the mare protecting her baby all those years before.

I should probably mention here that I originally began training in aikido as a way to help improve my horsemanship. I was fascinated by the core concepts of the art, primarily the ideas of entering into a conflict instead of fleeing from it, blending with the energy no matter how negative, and directing the situation to the most peaceful solution possible. I was also interested in the overall idea that aikido only works well when the practitioner is in control of him- or herself, as well as that the overall goal of the aikidoka (one who practices the art) is to make sure the attacker isn't harmed during an altercation. In other words, those who practice aikido must take care of their attacker, even though the attacker's intent may be to harm them.

When I first began training, I, like most new students, was flooded with the art's various techniques. I was taught how to move fluidly and how to strike and punch properly. I was also taught ukemi, the art of defending, or taking care of oneself. However, something I had read while doing my initial research prior to beginning formal training seemed to be missing.

Specifically, there wasn't much talk about or practice of the internal (and ultimately, external) quiet that is necessary to perform the art properly.

Most of my training in those early days focused on how to perform the techniques through strength and the control of my partner's joints. Of course, these too are important aspects. But as my training progressed, I assumed that the focus would eventually shift to the finer and more refined aspects of the art, the internal and external softness I had read so much about.

Unfortunately, however, those aspects were seldom talked about or practiced in our dojo; the style of aikido in which I had chosen to train was taught by instructors who focused on proper technique through total control of an opponent's body. They taught the way they themselves had been trained.

The techniques of aikido are extremely effective, regardless of how much finesse is used. Because of this effectiveness, the more muscle an aikidoka puts behind the technique, the less he or she can feel how the partner's body is responding to it and the higher the risk of injury to the partner. Over time, I noticed that our dojo was losing students because of the overall lack of sensitivity displayed during the performance of techniques, particularly by the higher-ranking students. In fact, of the dozen or so students who began their training around the same time I did, I am the only one who is still a practicing member of our dojo.

Many students quit after being injured while training with one of the higher-ranking students whose technique was absolutely flawless but whose feel was lacking. Many suffered broken fingers, hyper-extended elbows, concussions, sprained wrists, and injured knees. I ended up with a separated collarbone and a torn rotator cuff (among many other injuries), which I ultimately needed surgery to repair.

As time went on, the number of students dwindled to just a handful, then it went down to three, and finally, there were just two: me and one other. At that point, aikido classes were canceled; in order to continue training, the two of us were absorbed into the karate classes.

During the months the class list was dwindling, I was on the road doing horsemanship clinics, which gave me a chance to search out other dojos around the country. As luck would have it, I found myself training and studying with some of the top individuals in the art, people I had only heard and read about until then. As I launched into my training with these folks, I almost immediately began to experience the type of powerful softness that had been eluding me, not only in my aikido training, but in my horsemanship as well.

The first time I trained with someone who had a deep understanding of this powerful softness was in a small dojo on the West Coast. Sensei (the instructor) called on me, the visiting student, to help demonstrate a technique in front of the class. I was to throw an overhead strike downward toward the instructor's head, a motion similar to coming down with a knife or bottle. He would then perform the technique with me so the other students would know what he wanted them to practice.

The particular technique he was demonstrating was one in which I was fairly well versed. A version of a movement known as kokyunage, it was one I had grown to despise in my home dojo; it always ended up with me having a sore arm and shoulder as a result of the force exerted on both during the throw by the people with whom I was training.

As I lined up to administer the strike, I could feel the apprehension building. This is going to hurt, I thought to myself. I had heard stories of visiting students going into a new dojo and promptly being turned into punching bags by the sensei and other high-ranking students—a way to show off the "skill" of the dojo.

Sensei could see the apprehension in me. Heck, a blind man could have seen the apprehension in me. He exhaled, and then smiled. "Don't worry," he said so quietly that only I could hear. Then he nodded, which was a signal for me to throw the strike, which I did.

As I swung my hand downward toward his head, I braced myself for what I was sure was going to be the very painful lock, and then an equally painful throw. The strike came down with my full force behind it. As expected, Sensei moved slightly to his left, causing the strike to miss his head. Here it comes, I remember thinking. But instead of the painful lock I anticipated, Sensei gently caught my arm in the crook of his elbow and surprisingly, my arm just seemed to effortlessly move toward his body. My body followed my arm as he turned me slightly, and then for just a second, I felt weightlessly suspended in time and space. Then, I was suddenly but softly launched backward toward the mat. I went into the most perfect backward roll I believe I had ever done, which allowed me to pop right back up into a standing position, facing Sensei.

I had no idea how I had gotten there, or what Sensei had done that resulted in my acrobatics. All I knew was that it must have looked fantastic. As I stood there in my defensive stance facing Sensei, I wondered why the rest of the class wasn't clapping!

Sensei turned toward the class and began explaining what he had done. I immediately kneeled down (a sign of respect for the teacher), and as I looked at the faces of the students in the class, I slowly realized that the reason they weren't impressed with what had just happened was because it was nothing out of the ordinary for them. It was how they were being taught, with powerful softness. And just like that—as though someone flipped the switch on an enormous floodlight that only I could see—the thing that had been missing in my aikido, my horsemanship, and my life suddenly became very clear to me.

Over the next several years, I returned to that dojo whenever I was in the area, and found others around the country where the art was taught in a similar manner. Slowly but surely, I began to pick up on not only the subtleties of what was being taught, but also how the powerful softness I sought was actually being achieved.

I quickly came to realize that while there are a number of components and variables involved in developing the type of softness we are talking about here, two in particular made its achievement possible. The first is the overall development of what I would ultimately come to refer to as internal softness.

Internal softness is exactly what the words indicate: becoming soft from the inside, and then allowing that softness to extend through the rest of the body, both inside and out. This was the most difficult piece of the puzzle for me to comprehend, primarily because my awareness and understanding of it came much later in my training. But it was also because the idea was quite foreign to me; most of my instructors used different terms to describe basically the same concept. As a result, I found that for a while, I was trying to understand the words they were using instead of grasping the concept itself.

Before going further, I need to step back for just a second here and reiterate that in most forms of horsemanship, a tremendous amount of focus is put on riders developing softness in their hands. In fact, at one time or another, most of us have probably heard of getting a horse to follow a "feel." This particular idea or concept usually refers to a rider or handler gently directing the horse by means of a rope or rein that goes from the person's hand to the horse's head or mouth.

While this thought is certainly a very good one, and while it is also one that I have talked about and even taught over the years, the unfortunate part is that it sometimes stops short of taking into account the whole picture in regard to total softness. You see, by focusing on just softening the hands, which is what a lot of folks do, we are only taking into account one small part of the body: the hands. Not only that, but our hands are at the very end of our arms, as far away from the body as they can possibly get. So, while trying to soften the hands is certainly a good beginning to the process, I'm not sure how much total softness is actually being transferred to the horse if the rest of the body happens to be stiff or tense.

That being said, my training with some of the aikido masters I've mentioned helped me come to the realization that total softness doesn't come from the outside of the body. It comes from the inside. Also, there are two separate but equally important aspects to developing this internal softness. The first is the part that actually involves physically softening the inside of the body, which can be achieved through practicing certain relatively easy physical exercises. The second can be much more difficult for most folks to achieve because it involves the emotional facet of softness, a quiet and positive mind, which in turn has a tendency to enhance our overall physical softness.

The reason the emotional facet can be so difficult to achieve is that many people go through their everyday lives with fairly high levels of stress and concern for just about everything they do or are involved with. These folks generally put an equal amount of importance on all things in their lives, whether all things in their lives are actually important or not. For instance, if we were to assign our various daily activities or situations a value based on a numerical scale of importance from zero to ten, with zero meaning the activity or situation needs none of our energy or time and ten meaning the thing is an emergency that needs all of our attention and time, we might be surprised to find that most of us consistently run at about a six or a seven every day, and in almost all situations. For instance, forgetting to pick up milk at the store might carry the same importance as our car having a flat tire. Having a flat might have the same importance as seeing our son fall and skin his knee, and that might have the same importance as being cut off in traffic, which holds the same importance as our dog having an accident on the rug.

When there is so little variation in the level of importance of basic daily situations or activities, folks often find it very difficult to achieve a calm, quiet state of mind. This in turn can translate into internal strife and a lack of internal softness, not just with our horses, but with everything we do all day long.

Another thing that can get in the way of achieving internal softness is carrying a negative outlook into our daily activities. This negativity often includes the words we use as well as the types of interactions we have with those around us, both horse and human. Calling our horse derogatory names, for instance, in response to some unwanted behavior could fall into this category.

I suppose many folks reading this may scoff at the idea that the way we think and the words we use have anything to do with how the outside of our body responds (or doesn't respond) to our mind's request for softness when softness is needed. But the truth is, our body and our emotions operate as a unit, not as separate entities that can somehow be disconnected from one another. It's impossible for one to work in perfect harmony while the other is in perfect turmoil. When turmoil is present in one, it will be present in both. And when excess turmoil exists, especially over time, true softness can be very difficult, if not impossible, to develop.

As I continued to study and practice the intricacies of the internal and external softness I had been seeking for myself through my training in aikido, I found I was still only getting glimpses of its practical application during my work with horses. Sometimes, softness in my horses would show up as a slightly different feel in a lead rope or rein, or perhaps a horse I was working with might suddenly pick its foot up upon request with little or no effort, or quietly step over while tied at the hint of a touch from my hand. Sometimes, a transition would show up with my horse at a mere thought on my part; other times, it wouldn't.

Without question, these were all very positive steps in the direction I was trying to go, but they were hardly the kind of dramatic response I had seen and felt with my partners in the dojo. In the dojo, I was beginning to develop an ability to bring this type of powerful softness to bear so that my partner's entire body would suddenly give way with little more than a touch from a hand or arm. Then, almost magically, my partner would feel weight-less within whatever technique we were practicing. This weightlessness quickly turned into what one of my instructors referred to as unity, when two or more individuals become so connected internally that they become a single entity, both working off the same thought at the same time.

Still, developing that same, very specific feeling with horses on a rela-tively consistent basis had eluded me. That is, until the day I was helping a clinic participant whose horse had a trailer-loading issue. Or perhaps more accurately, what the horse had was a trailer-unloading issue. That is to say, the gelding would go into the trailer without too much fuss, but the only way he would leave it was if someone turned him around and led him out. It seemed nearly impossible for him to back out.

Normally, this wouldn't have been a problem for the owner, and in fact, she didn't know it was a problem until she bought a new trailer. Her previous trailer had been a small four-horse bumper-pull stock trailer with no divid-ers, so she had always just turned the horse around and led him out. But when she purchased a brand-new, special-ordered, two-horse slant-load trailer with living quarters and hauled her horse in it for the first time, she realized she had an issue!

After reaching her destination, she tried backing the 15.3-hand, 1,200-pound gelding out of the trailer, only to find that he was having none of it. Three hours later, she took the horse home without ever having unloaded him. Once there, she called a vet, had the gelding tranquilized, and eventually just sort of poured him out.

She then tried a number of things to help the horse get used to the idea of backing out, all of them sound and practical, but with limited success. By the time she came to the clinic, she was seriously considering selling her expensive new trailer and going back to a stock trailer of some kind so she could just turn him around.

We spent a little time with the gelding, a fairly quiet and amenable fellow all in all, and found that he would walk up to the back of the trailer without a problem. He'd put his front feet in the trailer when asked, stand, and then step back out. He could even put both front feet and one hind foot in the trailer and then back out. But as soon as he had all four feet in the trailer, he was stuck. The woman went in the trailer with him, and almost as soon as he stepped in with all four feet, she began tugging on the lead rope to get him to step back out. He wouldn't budge. She pushed on his chest with her hand, leaned on his neck with her shoulder, tapped his front legs with the lead rope, tugged on the lead rope again, and then used a combination of all of the above. Each time she added something, the horse just got stiffer and more determined to stand his ground. When nothing she did inside the trailer worked, she stepped out of the trailer with the lead rope in her hand and tried pulling him from behind. The gelding turned his head a bit in response to the pressure, but that was about it.

After a number of unsuccessful attempts, she turned to me, smiled, and handed me the rope. A slight chuckle came up from the couple of dozen folks there that day as spectators who had gathered around the trailer to see how we were going to resolve the gelding's issues.

This wasn't the first time I had seen a horse with this problem. In fact, it's actually more common than one might think. Sometimes this type of thing shows up as it had with this one, where once inside the trailer, the horse simply refuses to back out. Other times it shows up as a trailer loading issue, with the horse walking up to the back of the trailer and then refusing to get in. In both cases, the behavior is usually fear-based, and by spending a little time with the horse, working slowly, and limiting the amount of pressure used (or using the right amount of pressure at the right time), a horse can usually be talked into backing out of a trailer without too much effort.

But this guy was different. This was the first time I had seen a horse that was entirely determined to stand in one place until someone turned him around and led him out. Unfortunately, between the size of the horse and the limited space inside the trailer, turning him around wasn't an option. He was going to need to back out.

I smiled as I took the rope from the owner and stepped inside the trailer with the gelding. I petted him as I squeezed past him and moved to his head. Then, as gently as I could, I applied a little backward pressure on the rope similarly to what the owner had done originally, but with considerably less force. Oddly enough, on a number of occasions, just doing this one simple thing—backing off on the intensity of the pressure being used—had been enough to get a troubled horse to at least begin to start thinking about moving backward. Not this guy. Regardless of how little or how much pressure I applied, the feel coming back from him didn't change. I may as well have been leaning on a stone wall for all the responsiveness I was getting from him.

It was early May, and even though the weather was mild and all the windows and vents in the trailer were open, the sun was intense, and I could feel beads of sweat forming on my forehead and running down the middle of my back. The gelding was getting warm as well. His chest, flanks, shoulders, and even areas around his eyes were becoming dark with sweat. Every so often, a slight breeze would blow in through the open door, sending the faint odor of horse sweat past me and toward the front of the trailer.

I have to admit, these days I don't run into too many horse-related "problem" situations in which I am not confident that I can be of at least some help. That may sound boastful, but I don't intend it that way. After all, like most jobs, especially a job that one has done for a very long time, finding solutions to the same kinds of issues inherently becomes easier.

But as I stood there in the trailer, sweat running off both me and the horse, it became pretty clear that neither of us had any idea how we were going to get ourselves out of that predicament. I tried asking him to move backward with just the lead rope, and when that didn't work, I placed my hand on his nose and asked him to move. When that didn't work, I used my hand on his chest, and when that didn't work, I tried a combination of my hand on his chest while putting pressure on the lead rope. I tried gently rocking him back and forth to see if I could get him to take a step laterally one way or the other, as sometimes that can be enough to unlock both a horse's feet and his mind. None of that worked either.

Everything I had done to that point took less than five minutes, but I could already tell that getting him to think about moving backward was going to take a whole lot longer, if he thought about it at all. He was absolutely convinced that he wasn't going to be able to do it, and because of that, he wasn't willing to move in any direction other than forward.

If we had had more room, forward may have actually been an option because at least it would have been movement, and movement is something that we can direct. Even forward movement in situations like this can sometimes be turned into backward movement when handled correctly. But unfortunately, if I allowed him to go any farther forward inside the trailer, we wouldn't have room to work at all.

So there we stood.

I let out a long sigh, partially to fend off frustration and partially to let the horse know that even though the situation seemed insurmountable, I wasn't upset with him. As is almost always the case, as soon as I exhaled, the gelding seemed to relax, and exhaled as well. Then, simultaneously, he lowered his head and shifted his weight forward. I was standing almost directly in front of him, and as he shifted forward, he purposely placed his nose on my left hip, with the top of his head up near my shoulder. He made gentle contact, and then very intentionally began to roll his weight into me as though he were an elephant trying to push over a tree.

It's funny how the mind works. Almost as soon as I felt the gelding leaning into me, my first thought—and response—was to push back into him. I suppose this was partially because it's our natural instinct to push on things that push on us, and partially because I didn't want to get run over. Of course, pushing into a horse dead set on moving through, past, or over you is never a good idea, and I quickly came to my senses. However, I also didn't remove myself or get out of the horse's way. Instead, I stood my ground in a way similar to what I had done just a couple of weeks earlier during an aikido class.

In that particular class, we had been focusing on the internal elements of aikido. Specifically, how to blend with what seemed like an inordinate amount of force, pressure, or energy while at the same time giving positive and productive direction to that same force, pressure, or energy. During one exercise, several students lined up. Everyone in the line placed their hands on the shoulders of the person in front of them, with the exception of the person at the head of the line. That person turned and faced the line. Then, the second person in line, now face-to-face with the first, placed his or her hands on that person's shoulders. When Sensei gave the word, all of the people in the line, as a group, leaned into the person at the head of the line.

The first step of the exercise was that the person who was being leaned against engaged his or her center and then dropped to the floor to the point at which it was possible to hold the line without being moved or pushed over. Once that was accomplished, the next step was for that same person to soften internally while remaining physically stable externally.

Most of the folks in class that night were fairly well versed in the principles of developing internal softness, which consisted of breathing properly, keeping a quiet mind, and bringing to bear the remnants of a physical exercise we had done earlier that night, one that was designed to simultaneously soften the body from the inside out and enhance the power of the individual's center. It was at that point that something seemingly unbelievable became achievable. Once those principles were in place for the person at the head of the line (the one being leaned upon by as many as nine other people), that person was able to connect internally through that softness to each of the other individuals in the line.

Then, by doing little more than thinking about which direction he or she wanted the line to move, the individuals in the line would begin to feel that their bodies had started to match the softness coming from the inside of the person being leaned against. Further, they all ended up moving in the direction of that person's thought. Within seconds of everyone in the line softening and then tipping in the direction of the leader's thought, the line itself began to collapse and the people in it toppled like dominos.

Of course, we had also performed a number of similar exercises that evening in which the internal elements of the art were practiced, but for some reason, it was this one that came to mind as the horse and I stood together in the trailer. Possibly because the feel of the gelding leaning on me was so similar to the feel I had experienced when my fellow students had leaned on me that night when it was my turn at the head of the line.

Regardless, as the horse pushed into me with his head, I adjusted my stance slightly, sliding my left foot back for a bit more stability. Then, just as during the exercise, I softened from the inside while allowing the outside of my body to remain firm and constant, then dropped all my weight into my back foot, using my back leg as an anchor. The horse initially responded with more pressure, but then very quickly, a ripple of a relaxation passed through his entire body. That relaxation lasted only a couple of seconds before he stiffened and begin pushing again. When he did, the push was heavier and considerably more intense; it felt as though it started at his hind feet, came up through his topline, over his withers, through his neck, across his poll, and directly into his forehead and nose, transferring the push into my shoulder and hip.

Normally, this kind of pressure would have been enough to dislodge me from my stance. After all, the horse was much bigger, heavier, and stronger than I could even think about being. But it didn't! Instead, I could feel all of the pressure from the horse's push moving from my hip and shoulder into my body, where it was absorbed and then transferred down my back leg and into the floor of the trailer, causing me to be even more stable than I had been in the beginning.

The horse continued to lean, and I did my best to remain soft and stable. After just a couple of minutes, I could feel the push that had been so strong just seconds before begin to dissipate. The change was almost imperceptible at first, and I'm sure that had I been pushing back, I would have never felt it. But as it was, I was basically just standing in one spot in the most stable stance I could find and allowing the gelding to push against me—just like that hitch rail that I described earlier. Like a hitch rail that remains neutral while a horse pulls against it, I was basically doing my best to do the same thing with opposite pressure: remaining neutral while the horse was pushing against me.

And just like when a horse pulls against something that isn't moving and the only way he finds a release is to go toward it, in this case, the horse found his release by moving away from the thing he was pushing against—namely, me. The pressure the gelding was applying to my shoulder and hip dropped off very subtly at first, almost imperceptibly. But the longer we stood together, and the softer I tried to remain, the softer and more willing he became to move in the direction I was suggesting, while at the same time maintaining his connection with me.

It was the kind of connection I had felt numerous times in the dojo, but this was the very first time I had ever felt it at that level with a horse. The two of us stayed physically connected, his forehead on my shoulder and his nose on my hip, as each of us softened into one another. My level of aware-ness of what was going on with the horse's body was like nothing I had ever felt before. It became a conversation that took me a little time to figure out. There were questions from him and answers from me, and questions from me and answers from him. At the risk of sounding anthropomorphic, the conversation felt a little something like this:

Could you shift a little bit this way?
I don't think so. But I might be able to go that way.
That way would be fine.
And then he would move that way.
I need to go to the right a little, I'd feel him saying.
Let's settle for a second, I'd hint.
Settling might be good, came back from him.

And within this quiet, supportive conversation, movement that had seemed impossible just a few minutes earlier began to slowly show itself. The movement began with the gelding simply relaxing his body from his nose to his tail. Then small shifts of weight began to develop, side to side at first. Slowly, within the sideways movement, the slight shifts of weight back-ward began to increase. Soon, the sideways movement lessened and the backward movement grew, until the big gelding eventually took one very tiny step toward the back of the trailer with his right front foot.

Without losing our connection or pushing him to move more, I gently petted him on his cheek and neck while continuing to work the softness that had developed between us. By this time, he seemed almost completely relaxed and willing, although unsure, to try to start working himself backward.

Soon, another small step showed up, this time with his left front foot. Then he took another tiny step with his right front, and then his left hind. He stopped and stiffened slightly as though realizing for the first time that he was moving in the direction he didn't think he could go. He offered to come forward by leaning into me, but very quickly gave that up, softened, and shifted backward once again. He hesitated for several seconds, then—with a deep, long sigh—took a big step backward with his right hind foot. When he did, the foot ended up at the very back of the trailer floor, as far back as he could have stepped without actually stepping out. That step was followed by a step backward with his left front foot, then his left hind and finally his right front.

He was now perched at the very back of the trailer with both hind feet partially hanging off the edge of trailer floor. He very gently leaned into me again. This time, it felt like he needed a little support rather than wanted to move forward. He let out another sigh. Several seconds passed, then he shifted his weight in order to get himself in better balance. Finally, as though he had been doing it all his life, he very deliberately stepped out of the trailer with his right hind foot. He hesitated again, and then slid his left hind foot out. He quickly but softly shuffled both front feet out the trailer and then, just like that, his whole body was outside the trailer.

The folks who were watching broke into excited but quiet applause, and the gelding looked over at them as though wondering what all the fuss was about.

I led the gelding away from the trailer; made a couple of small, quiet circles; then took him back. He loaded right up and then, with the same type of soft but meaningful encouragement, he backed out a second time. He and I repeated this several times until he could literally load and unload himself without a hint of worry. By the time I gave him back to his owner, loading and unloading him was so easy that you would have never known there was an issue in the first place.

Only later would it dawn on me that this was the first time I could remember consciously using the kind of "full-body" internal softness that we've been discussing here. Prior to this particular horse leaning into me, I had been doing pretty much what we all do in similar situations—the thing we've all been taught and on which we spend most of our time focusing. That is, trying to develop softness and, consequently, movement, through our hands alone. In other words, getting the horse to "follow the feel" that we spoke about earlier, in which that "feel" begins and ends with our hands.

I had used my hands on the lead rope to try to direct him backward. When that didn't work, I used my hand on his nose, and when that didn't work I used my hand on his chest, and then I used my hands on both the lead rope and his chest. Everything I had done to give him direction had been coming specifically from my hands, arms, and upper body, with the inside of me and the rest of my body inadvertently disconnected from the task. Ultimately, I had just been working on the surface, using mechanics and strength and trying to elicit a "feel" response. And the gelding initially ended up responding in kind.

In tapping into this internal, and ultimately, full-body softness within myself, I found that not only did the gelding become much less resistant to the idea of moving backward in a shorter period of time, but he also became much more receptive to the idea of working with me to find a solution to the issue at hand. I believe it was the kind of unity my aikido instructor was striving to pass along to his students in the dojo, the same kind of unity that certain well-known horsemen, and even lesser-known, such as Walter Pruit (the Old Man with whom I had been lucky to spend time with as a youngster) were trying to help people understand. It is that intangible within ourselves that allows for the tangible to come through in everything we do, whether with horses or in our everyday lives.

For me, working toward developing this type of internal softness has since opened doors to a level of communication with horses that I wasn't sure was possible just a few short years ago. Perhaps even more critically, however, it has opened up a much deeper awareness into that communication, which I have found to be almost more important than the communication itself.

What I mean by this (and speaking strictly for myself) is that I have always been amazed at the incredible subtlety that horses use to communicate with one another. For instance, I don't know how many times in our own little herd here at home I've seen Tuff, the patriarch, elicit movement from one or more of the other horses without so much as a sideways glance or even the flick of an ear.

Just the other day, I was doing some work in a pen occupied by Tuff and four of our other horses, including my two main clinic horses, Rocky and Cooper. I had just finished up what I was doing and turned to look at the horses, all of whom were standing relatively close to one another over near the water tank. It was a warm afternoon and they were standing quietly, lazily swishing their tails at the flies buzzing around their hind legs. Nothing seemed out of the ordinary or troublesome for any of the horses, including Tuff. Yet, as I stood watching, Cooper, our roan gelding who was standing close but just on the outside of the group, quietly but very deliberately turned an eye and ear toward Tuff.

Tuff's expression and posture had not changed at all. His head was low, his eyes were half-closed, and his thick tail rhythmically flicked from one side to the other. Cooper continued to keep a wary eye on him. After about thirty seconds, he stepped away, all the while maintaining his observation of Tuff. Rocky, who had been standing next to Cooper but between him and Tuff, had shown no signs that anything was out of the ordinary. That is, until Cooper moved a good twenty feet away from his herd mates and came to a stop. At that point, Rocky turned his eye and ear toward Tuff in the same manner as Cooper, but instead of immediately moving away, he questioningly turned and looked at the little dun gelding. Again, Tuff had not moved or shown any outward signs to elicit that kind of response from Rocky, or at least, none that I could see. Yet there was no question that Rocky seemed to be feeling something from him.

Rocky turned briefly and looked at Cooper, then back at Tuff. Then, without any hesitation whatsoever, he turned and walked to where Cooper was standing. Rocky took up the same position next to Cooper that he had been in when they both were standing with the herd. Then, in unison, with exactly the same expression on their face, both geldings turned and looked at Tuff. Tuff had still not changed position or attitude as far as I could see, but it was clear there was some kind of communication going on. Rocky and Cooper stood there for several seconds, ears up and eyes alert. After those seconds passed, and as if responding to some cue only they could see, both horses, again in unison, relaxed and turned their heads forward.

For me, three very important elements had transpired between these horses. The first was that there was no question but that Tuff seemed very soft, both inside and out. The second was that he seemed to be in some way deliberately communicating with both Cooper and Rocky, an interaction so small it couldn't be detected. The third, and possibly the most important, element was that Cooper and Rocky were able to receive and understand what Tuff was saying, and to respond accordingly.

So when I talk about there being deeper awareness into the communication, I am speaking about the presence of these three elements between the parties involved before the communication has even begun: internal and external softness, deliberate and clear communication, and the ability of the second party to receive and understand the information being sent.

For most horses, this type of communication appears to be second nature, easy to project and receive. But for humans, or at least the majority of us, it seems necessary to really work at just trying to understand it, much less get good enough to use it effectively. I think the main reason the understanding and performing of this type of communication can be so difficult for us is that it begins with a quiet mind and internal and external softness within at least one of the parties involved, and ends with a common goal having been reached, a new behavior having been learned, or an unwanted behavior having been redirected. Our struggle to quiet our mind and our lack of knowledge and experience in developing and using internal softness can, and often does, get in our way.

Still, I had first become aware of this type of communication with another human while working with one of my aikido instructors who had chosen me as his uke (training partner) during demonstrations. He would extend his hand, an indication that he wanted me to take his wrist so he could demonstrate a technique. In each case, as I reached out to take his wrist, but just prior to actually making contact with him (and without knowing ahead of time which direction he wanted me to go or even what technique we were going to demonstrate), I could already feel my body moving in the direction he ultimately wanted me to go. He had somehow made a connection and influenced my movement without touching me, which, of course, made the actual technique virtually effortless for both of us.

For me, that is what true softness is all about when it comes to working with horses: being able to develop a connection with the horse through softness, in which movement can ultimately become effortless for both the horse and the rider. Not only that, but when offered correctly, that same effortlessness can be achieved even when one of the parties puts up resistance!

I have found in my own quest that the development of a quiet mind and internal softness is a great beginning—a reliable way to travel in the direction of developing that effortlessness of movement and communication between horse and human. However, I have also come to understand over the years that there are a few other aspects to that development that are equally, if not more, important—aspects that we seldom if ever think about, and in many cases aren't even aware of. Still, once understood, practiced, and implemented, these aspects, along with the others we've already talked about, can make all the difference in the world as to how our horses, and even the people around us, ultimately respond to us. And even more importantly, how we respond to them.

To be really good at it, and I mean really good at it, softness must be practiced in all aspects of life—in everything we do, all the time, without exception.

Thoughts on Connection, Feel, and Softness

Michelle Scully

Connection. I first met Mark through my friend Stephanie. Steph had attended several of his clinics, and she was impressed. My clinic experience at that point was pretty negligible, but I respect her opinion, so I signed up for a clinic she was hosting at her place. I grew up riding backyard horses in a backyard kind of way, which meant I made do with whatever tack I had. It was just "Get on and go," whether from a fence or a tree or riding doubles—it was always function over form. Learning about horse "training" and clinics was new to me, but I've always been a student of life, so I was game.

Game, but more than a little afraid when Steph told me that clinics also have auditors. It was hard for me to put myself and my rough-and-tumble skills out there for general consumption, but I trusted her, and rode in the first morning spot. Mark made things easy. He's a pretty personable guy and just slightly funny, and he quickly helped me feel more at ease. Over the years, I've come to know and appreciate how his low-key demeanor helps people get past that awkward phase and move on to the real horsemanship part.

Connection was one of the words that kept coming up in riding with Mark. Prior to that, I'd thought connection just meant that you were still connected to your horse when your ride was done, but this was something different. Over the years since that first clinic, I've spent a lot of time thinking about connection and trying to be part of it rather than "pursuing it" in the way we humans seem to do when we're on a mission to "do" something. We do a lot of things to horses—lead them, drag them, spur them, you name it—but partnering up with them seems to be a lot harder for us to envision, let alone do. Now, when I think of connection, it's come to seem like a good marriage—two energies uniting and blending in a common purpose.

It's much easier to do things to or at a horse and to preempt his input by being so engrossed in our own agenda that we're not interested in what he brings to the party. We get impatient waiting on a horse, we rush through our presentation of what we want him to do, and are often frustrated when he "doesn't get it," rather than setting up a situation in a way that the horse can figure out for himself. One of the biggest things I've learned from watching Mark over the years is that any disconnect or frustration with the horse is usually operator error (mea culpa!). He's way too nice to say it, but I've figured that out for myself. If I'm not presenting my intention with clarity, it's highly unlikely that my horses are going to know what I'm asking them for.

I had a bad wreck several years ago and wasn't able to ride for quite a while. I was so grateful when I could be around my horses again, and just be in the peacefulness of their presence. One thing I learned in this enforced state of semi-quietness was just exactly how noisy my brain was most of the time. As I was forced to move more slowly due to my physical limitations, I realized that my brain could move more slowly, too, and quiet down a bit. I realized that the human state (or at least mine) seems to be about going full-bore, a hundred miles per hour, and then taking all that rushing-forward energy and banging it into our horses when we decide "Okay, now it's time to ride . . . train . . . or whatever." As much as I really just wanted to ride, that period of time taught me a great life lesson in the need to quiet my mind and enter the horse's energy in a more peaceful way rather than the jerky "start and stop" kind of thing I am afraid I probably did way too much of the time.

Mark always says that horsemanship is life. Our lives are pretty different, but life is life no matter where you are, and always provides plenty of opportunities for practice. He's a renowned horseman who is also a life-long student of aikido; I teach biology at our local college and grocery shop for two teenage boys and a husband. In all those efforts, there are opportunities to seek clarity and to quiet the mind. I guess if I had to sum up what connection means to me, it's that I'm seeking to be united with my horse in a partnership where both of our thoughts count.

One of the biggest reasons I fell in love with my husband was because he is a great swing dancer; we really got to know one another by dancing together. I've spent a lot of time thinking about the difference between a good dance partner and somebody you just don't want to dance with. I see that same kind of partnership in creating connection with my horse: he allows me to ride on his back and I don't denigrate that trust by ignoring his physical or mental wellbeing. I'm a respectful presence who realizes that our partnership is a dance—our thoughts and movements blend together to a place where we both hear the same music. At the end of the day, we're glad we danced together.

It's kind of funny, because I often look back to how I rode as a kid and wonder if I've really progressed, or am just finding my way back. As kid, my horse was my partner, and I always rode her with the thought that we were going on a great adventure together. We were connected all the way. My goal now is to ride my horses just a little bit more like I did when I was five.

Feel. I first heard about feel years ago when I bought the book *True Horsemanship Through Feel* by Bill Dorrance and Leslie Desmond. They talked about things that I'd never heard anyone talk about before, but it was a way of interacting with horses that intrigued me. Working with somebody like Mark, up close and first-hand, I had my first experience with feel in action. He talked about timing, footfall, and knowing where the horse's feet are at all times, and setting up what you're asking of the horse to coincide with these attributes. Given where I was starting from, it was a lot for me, and sometimes I felt overwhelmed, wondering if I'd ever develop that skill. I took comfort in the realization that one of the things I like about myself is that I am empathetic and fairly sensitive to nuance. I just hoped those traits would translate into my work with horses. Again, I thought back to the riding I'd done as a kid, and it was all on instinct and feel. Somehow, "growing up" got me a little off track from that internal sensor I had when I was little.

I also took comfort in the fact that at least now I knew the difference between feel for and with a horse and just getting by. We tend to be always in a rush to "get things done," and that was another thing I learned from Mark about feel. You have to take the time it takes to be with a horse. That means that you set your agenda by the wayside and are fully present when you are with a horse. Your head can't be somewhere outside the round pen or arena, thinking about other things.

When horses do that, we tend to get all over them, but I think we do it ourselves more often than we'd like to admit. It's easy for us to get a plan locked in our minds and sometimes, it makes it easy to miss the small things that really matter and that lead us to feel with horses and in life. I've learned that you need to give yourself leeway to make mistakes, as long as you make them with grace and good will. When you're coming from a good place to start with, horses (and children) are very willing to give you the benefit of the doubt if you come back and try again. As with raising children, sometimes you blow it, and a heartfelt apology is always the best answer. I feel my way through life, motherhood, and horses, too.

True feel is an all-over thing, a beautiful equation of connection, balance, timing, and heart. Feel is like a great conversation between the rider and the horse. It's not one-sided and it's not an argument. It's a conversation that both parties enjoy having. One of the most beautiful things I've ever seen is a true horseman asking a horse to move out through the feel he transmits via a lead rope or a rein. It's all in the hands: the ask, the direction, the promise that hand is giving the horse. It says, "If you go there with me, I promise you won't regret it." In *True Horsemanship Through Feel,* Dorrance says, "Getting by is what so many people end up thinking is all right because they haven't had the opportunity to see how good it can be when a horse is operating through feel." You may start out not knowing anything about feel, but when you watch a true horseman use feel to work with a horse, you'll definitely know it when you see it. It's a beautiful thing and something I strive for. It's a lifelong process, but I'm working my way there.

Softness. Mark was the first person I heard make the distinction between softness and lightness. I was at a point at which distinctions like that were starting to sink in. In one of his videos, he uses an illustration of two horses being ridden, one with softness and one with lightness, and I could actually see the difference he was talking about. We see a lot of horses that are highly trained and respond almost instantaneously to the smallest ask. What I hadn't noticed before is that sometimes, signs came along with that: ear pinning, bit-chewing, tail-swishing or -clamping. I hadn't been in a position to put words to it before, but now it was making sense. Some horses are trained within an inch of their lives, but they're not really digging it. They are going through the motions, but their outsides and insides aren't in unity.

When my boys were little, I read books about raising kids. I am a book person by nature and was sure I didn't know anything at all, and worried about their survival. At the same time, I was attempting to train a two-year-old gelding I'd recently purchased and was also reading horsemanship books like crazy. It wasn't too long after that I threw my kid-raising books away. There's a lot to be said for getting horses (and kids) to come along with you by buying into what you're presenting.

To me, softness means unity between how a horse feels on the inside and the outside, and that he's engaged in the process. He's part of the process, not just a vehicle for some kind of activity to be accomplished by commandeering his physical skills. Internally, the horse has accepted what you've offered because he has developed confidence in himself and in you and trusts what you're bringing to the party. That confidence develops through connection, consistency, and feel.

Externally, softness develops in a horse that is physically well, without underlying physical issues that make it difficult for him to move comfortably. Softness develops in a horse that is ridden by a rider who has an awareness of how important balance and timing are. Put all that together and you have a horse that is set up for softness. When you take the inside (which you've established by offering connection and feel) and the outside (which is physically able to do all that is asked) and put them together, you get a happy, calm horse that actually feels good about what you're doing together. You're partners.

When you watch a horse and rider move together with softness, it's a powerful thing. You can tell the difference almost immediately, even if you didn't know you were looking for a difference. A horse that's soft can move on a thought—as though the rider says, "Let's go over there," and off they go; their movements seem united and effortless, almost like there's a float in them. It's a beautiful thing to see.

Initial Contact 4

There are things in life that we experience and, for some inexplicable reason, they just seem to stick with us forever. A particular odor, a certain song, a specific event, or perhaps even a combination of all of the above fit into that category. Like a lot of folks, I, too, have experiences that have stuck with me over the years, and when triggered by some present-day familiarity, are suddenly thrust to the forefront of my consciousness.

One such event occurred about fifteen years ago while I was in California for a series of clinics. A few of us had gone out to dinner following the last day of one of the clinics, and just as we had finished dinner and were heading for the door, a tall, slim gentleman with graying hair and a quick smile came in. Carly, one of the clinic participants, went to the man and gave him a hug and kiss. She then took him by the arm and ushered him over to me.

"Mark," she said with a smile, "this is my husband, Chris."

Carly had mentioned Chris a time or two during the clinic, but only to say he was her long-suffering "horse husband," not really into riding but happy to clean up and feed when she was out of town or unable to get away from work at a decent hour; he would also pet them on occasion and chip in when the ever-present bills that her four horses generated came in.

"Hello, Chris," I said as I offered my hand. "I've heard a lot about you."

"Not all bad, I hope!" he quipped as he took my hand and shook it.

I must admit I was taken completely by surprise at the feel I got from that handshake. There was a quality to it that I had seldom, if ever, experienced. Rather than the tight, non-feeling, and non-forgiving squeeze so many folks use, Chris's handshake was soft, but very connected—even powerful.

The second he took my hand, my mind immediately snapped back to a picture from my past. Well, to say it was a picture isn't quite accurate. A series of pictures flashed before my eyes—like one of those movie trailers, the ones where they're trying to show as many rapid-fire glimpses into the movie's story line as possible in the shortest amount of time.

Random visions of Walter, the Old Man from my childhood, as he petted this horse or that, picked up a lead rope, set down a bucket, picked up a scoop shovel, shifted his truck, and patted me on the shoulder for a job well done. Then, just as quickly as the images appeared, they were gone.

"Carly told me she had a great time, and learned a lot." Chris said, with what seemed to be a kind, ever-present smile. We gently broke off our handshake.

"She and Cracker did very well," I replied, referring to Carly and her horse, a fifteen-hand palomino gelding who sported the unusual color of a saltine.

One of the other ladies came up, gave Chris a hug, and began talking with him as we made our way out the door and into the relative darkness of the parking lot. We stopped under the flickering glow of a streetlight to say our good-byes and finish our conversations. After a short time, we drifted our separate ways. Carly, Chris, and I, along with the woman who had hugged Chris in the restaurant, headed in the same direction as we made our way to our vehicles.

"So what does Chris do for a living?" I asked Carly while Chris and the woman walked ahead of us. I was curious about what kind of job could nurture the kind of feel Chris was able to generate by simply shaking hands.

"He's an orthopedic surgeon," she smiled. "One of the best in L.A. He specializes in shoulders."

"I see."

It made perfect sense. Someone who needed his hands to be capable of both delicate and intricate work, yet strong enough to cut through bone and manipulate muscle and tendon would no doubt carry those qualities in the grip he would use to shake hands. If he were good at his work—which Chris was—this was something he would use not only in the operating room, but in everything he did.

It got me thinking about my own handshake, and the amount of muscle, pressure, and force I used when I shook someone's hand. Like so many others (both men and women), I was taught at an early age to look someone in the eye and shake hands firmly. Over the years, that idea had somehow morphed into me thinking that the "firmness" I used should directly correlate to the amount of firmness or pressure with which the other person responded. As a result, more than once, I would respond to an overly zealous or strong handshake with one of my own.

In fact, a strong grip was what I used to shake Chris's hand, at least initially. However, when he remained soft but connected with his hand in the midst of my unfeeling squeeze, I found myself almost instinctively switching and trying to match the feel he was using. It was a moment I could have very easily forgotten almost as soon as it occurred, or perhaps might not have noticed. I probably would have, had it not been for those pictures that flooded my consciousness as the two of us made contact.

I suppose the thing that can be so frustrating about how the mind works is how one piece of information can be taken in and suddenly, an entire series of seemingly unrelated information is triggered and brought to our awareness. This was what had happened for me that evening, and I remember driving back to my trailer that night trying to understand the correlation between what I had felt in Chris's handshake and all of those pictures from my past that it had conjured up.

Of course, looking back on the situation with over fifteen more years of experience, the connection seems obvious. But that night, trying to ease my way through the ceaseless L.A. traffic and at the same time make sure I didn't miss the exit that would eventually get me back to where my trailer was, the link between the two escaped me.

Then, several years later, something else occurred that brought the entire situation to the forefront of my consciousness. I was visiting a friend who is very accomplished in the martial arts; he holds a fourth-degree black belt in aikido, as well as black belts in two other arts. We were driving through town on our way to lunch when he suddenly remembered that he had to pick something up at the dojo where he trains and teaches. We made a detour off the main road and a few minutes later, were at the dojo.

Off and on that morning, we had discussed the intricacies of a certain aikido technique that I had been struggling with during my own training. As he parked the car in front of the dojo, he invited me in so that we might go over a couple of the things we had been talking about. I eagerly agreed and a few minutes later, the two of us, in street clothes and stocking feet, were standing on the mat.

"Okay," he said. "I'll take hold of you and you go ahead and perform the technique."

I nodded and offered my hand so that he could take hold of my wrist, which would initiate my performance of the technique. However, almost as soon as he touched me, and before I could even think about taking him into the technique, he released his grip.

"There's your problem," he said with a knowing smile.

I stopped and looked at my arm, which was still suspended in front of me pretty much right where I had offered it to him. He said nothing, so I looked at my stance, thinking maybe he saw something in the way I was standing that could have been causing my issue. He was quiet. I looked back up at him.

"What?" I questioned.

He pointed at my arm. "Your initial contact."

"You're making contact with me," I said with a hint of protest in my voice.

"That's the thing a lot of students have trouble understanding," he said flatly. "We are actually making contact with each other. I may be initiating it, but once we come together, the connection is both of our responsibilities, and because you are the one performing the technique, the majority of the feel of the technique falls to you."

He asked me to take hold of his wrist, just as he had done with me. I did, and he performed the technique. He exerted very little effort and I went to the mat fairly easily, completely aware of the moves that he was making that got me there, as well as the moves that I needed to make in order to get to the mat safely.

He then asked me to get back on my feet and take his wrist again, which I did. This time, almost as soon as I made contact with him, he put a feel in the arm that I was holding extremely similar to the feel in Chris's handshake. I quickly found that any excess tension I might have been holding in my body just seemed to completely evaporate. In that split second of what I would ultimately call total softness between the two of us, an opening was created in me that allowed my friend to not only perform the technique effectively, but also allowed him to direct my body in a most effortless manner. In the blink of an eye, I was on the mat. Unlike the first time he performed the technique, I really had no idea how I got there!

"Most people think it's the quality of the technique that gets your partner effectively to the mat," he smiled as I got to my feet, "when it's actually the quality of that initial contact that does it."

Standing there in the dojo, my friend then had me close my eyes as he touched my shoulder a number of times. He mentioned that by closing my eyes, it would be easier to feel the difference in how my body responded to the various touches he offered. Each time he touched, he would ever-so-slightly change the way he made contact. I was amazed at how dramatically my body responded to each touch, even though the feel did not seemed to change much. In other words, if we put the amount of physical pressure he was using to make contact with me on a scale from zero to ten, with zero being no pressure, each of his touches consistently ranged from between a .5 on that scale to a 1.5. Yet each touch had a noticeable impact on the way my body responded.

At will, he could touch me with very light contact, say, a .5 on the scale, and easily cause me to want to brace against him. Yet he could then touch me with a 1.5 and effortlessly move me all over the room, had he chosen to do so. Then he would switch and touch me with a .5 and immediately, I would feel that effortlessness of movement, while the 1.5 would create a brace.

"It's the willingness to blend with your partner that creates the feel you want in that initial contact," he said as he touched my shoulder over and over, each time creating the exact feel that he was seeking from me.

"We think that a touch is a touch is a touch, and contact is contact is contact." He touched me in such a way that it felt as though his finger stopped dead at my shoulder. My body ever so slightly braced against it. "But it isn't." He touched me again and it felt as though his finger went right through my shoulder. My body gently swayed at the contact he made.

"Technique is important," he said as I opened my eyes. "But unless the initial contact is right, technique is just technique. It's the quality of the initial contact that creates the magic."

As if someone had turned on a giant searchlight—the kind they use at movie premieres and the like—the connection between what I felt with Chris's handshake that night at the restaurant, and why images of the Old Man had flooded over me suddenly, and very clearly, was illuminated. It had been the similarity in the feel of how both men made their initial, physical contact, and the corresponding effect that contact had!

I couldn't even begin to count how many times I had watched the Old Man touch a horse, or pick up a shovel, or reach for the door handle of his pickup truck, or perform any number of seemingly mundane, everyday tasks, and always use what appeared to be the exact same soft quality in his hands. This was true regardless of whether or not the thing he was touching was a living breathing animal or person, or an inanimate object, like a gate latch or the handle on the old water pump.

It was interesting for me to realize that, while I was usually mindful of how I was using my hands, or more specifically, the feel in my hands, after I made contact with something, I couldn't recall very many instances in which I had been mindful of how I made my initial contact. Granted, there were the occasions when, dealing with an extremely sensitive or troubled horse, I would intentionally slow things way down as I picked up a rein or lead rope or otherwise made contact. But if the truth were known, I'd have to admit that in most other situations, I just wasn't as attentive as I could have been to making sure I used the same quiet deliberateness in my approach or contact.

It was an eye-opener for me, to say the least, and from that point forward, I made a commitment to myself to practice mindfulness in the way I used my hands, not just with horses, but in everything I did and everything I touched. It all began with me learning how to pick things up—a rein, a cup, a manure fork—using only the muscles that were needed to effectively grasp and manipulate the object. I was quickly amazed at just how often I caught myself using significantly more muscle to do something simple than was actually needed.

Many was the time that, in my haste to get something done fast, or move something quickly, I would find myself carelessly grasping an item with little or no thought as to how I was doing it. Only after I had taken hold of it and tried to do something with the item would I realize just how much excess tension there was in my hands, arms, shoulders, and oftentimes, throughout my entire body. I'd find that I'd have to physically stop what I was doing, or getting ready to do, and take a minute to mindfully release the tension in my body that had been caused simply by the way I made contact with an object.

I must say that one of the most disheartening things for me during this time was to come to the realization that the kind of tension I was recognizing in myself was tension that up until then had gone completely unnoticed. Well, unnoticed by me, that is. I'm quite certain the horses I had been working with were very aware of it, and that was enough reason for me to want to find a way to change the way I was doing things.

The sad thing is, had someone told me prior to all of this that I was generating unnecessary tension in my body simply by the way I was making contact with things around me, I probably would have dismissed the observation. After all, I had spent a great deal of time, most of my life in fact, in pursuit of softness, and I was pretty sure I understood what it was, how to achieve it, and how to implement it.

So, on one hand, to find that I was actually a little further from my ultimate goal of true softness than I had led myself to believe was a bit disheartening. But on the other hand, it was clear that a whole new realm of possibilities was being offered just behind this particular door. There was no question that I had only just cracked it open. In order to see what was behind it, I would need to find a way to swing it open a little wider. But first, I had to come to grips with the idea that, like so many other horse folks, I had gotten stuck in the thought that softness is what happens after we make contact with our horse.

Certainly, that is a component, but what my friend had shown me in the dojo that day was that softness is (or should be) generated way before we make contact, and then is carried through the initial touch and into the connection, which can ultimately create the type of total unity we are searching for.

I had found that my efforts to be mindful when first making contact with things I touched was a great start in the development of initial-contact softness, and for the most part, I was beginning to see a difference in some of the horses I was working with when I applied it. But as time went on, I also began to get the feeling that something was still missing. You see, when working with my friend in the dojo, the softness he generated seemed to come very naturally to him, as if it were no effort for him at all. But I found that I had to really focus on what I was doing in order to develop the same sort of softness in myself. Not only that, but the type of feel in my hands that I was trying to develop in order to achieve initial-contact softness was fleeting, at best.

Then, as luck would have it, something happened that just seemed to bring all the pieces of the puzzle together. My friend, the one who had introduced me to the concept of initial-contact softness in the first place, gave me a DVD that had been filmed at an aikido seminar he had attended. It was a large seminar, at which a number of leading aikido practitioners had gathered to help teach various techniques and philosophies to the students in attendance.

I had begun to watch the DVD a number of times, but each time, had been unceremoniously interrupted by something that seemed to need my immediate attention. As a result, over a year and a half had passed before I finally got a chance to watch it all the way through.

There was a great deal of information in the DVD to be sure, but it wasn't the physical demonstrations that helped me understand the piece of the puzzle I seemed to be missing. Rather, it was something one of the instructors said just prior to beginning his class. As the section of the DVD dedicated to Frank Duran Sensei's demonstration faded on the screen, he bowed to his class and said simply, "Let us practice kindness today."

Those five words almost immediately helped me understand internally something that, until then, I had only recognized as an external act. For the first time, I could see that endeavoring to make contact as softly as we can through the mechanical act of reaching and touching is obviously an important aspect of what we are talking about here. But the kind of initial-contact softness that my friend had shown me isn't just about the way we externally touch something or someone. It is the kind of intent that we put into it.

I could see how, in my quest to develop a soft touch or feel when making contact with something (specifically my horses), my focus had been on the way the contact felt externally. Specifically, the speed at which I made contact; the amount of pressure I used during and after the touch; and the amount of tension in my hand, wrist, and arm while I was doing it. What I hadn't been paying attention to was the intent that I was putting behind it in the first place.

It was at that point I began to understand that initial-contact softness wasn't really so much about the physical or external contact at all. Rather, it was about the internal feel with which that contact was initiated. And what better internal feel to initiate external contact than kindness? As simple as this one little aspect may sound, for me it was a major turning point, not only in my horsemanship, but also in my life.

The very next day after watching the DVD, I began to apply the words that Duran Sensei so eloquently used when addressing his class: "Let us practice kindness today." The response from the horses I came in contact with was immediate and profound, and included the responses I received from my own horses. That morning when I went out to catch Rocky and Mic, the two horses I was traveling with, I carried with me the idea of presenting kindness not just in the way I made contact with them, but in everything I did leading up to that contact.

I picked up their halters with the idea of kindness in mind; I walked across the yard carrying the same feel with me. When I opened the gate to the pasture they were in, I tried to do it as kindly as possible. As I headed in their direction, both horses seemed to take notice.

Now, I should point out that my horses have really never been difficult to catch, and in fact most of the time when I go to get them, even when we're on the road, they will meet me at the gate. So I halfway expected, and even kind of took for granted, that they would willingly stand while I approached and caught them.

What I wasn't expecting was the subtle difference in the expressions on both of their faces as I approached, which was one of soft acceptance, and that when I placed the nosebands of the halters in front of them in preparation to gently sliding the halters over their noses, both horses very quietly but deliberately placed their noses in the halters for me. If someone had seen me catch my horses the day before, and then watched me catch them on that day, they may not have seen much of a difference. In fact, I'm not sure I would have noticed much of an outward difference had I not been paying attention.

What I noticed was how my horses seemed to feel, not only about being caught and haltered, but simply how they responded when I reached out to touch them. It's hard to explain, other than to say that there was a quiet availability to them that seemed to be a bit deeper than anything I had experienced from either of them in the past. That feel stayed with us as we left the pen and went to the trailer, where I groomed and saddled them both. Eventually, I led them to the arena where our work for the day was waiting for us.

We were in the middle of a three-day clinic in the Midwest, and there were two horses (and riders) at the clinic who were struggling with the concept of being soft when contact was made with the bit through the reins. The previous day, we had worked with each horse-and-rider pair on a couple of things that I thought might help; while progress was made, it wasn't as much as I had hoped for. On this day, however, when the horses and riders came in, the idea of practicing kindness was in the forefront of my mind.

As I began talking with the first rider, whose horse wasn't a heck of a lot softer than he had been the day before, I approached and asked her if it would be all right if I took hold of the reins. The rider was mounted and readily agreed. Standing on the horse's left side, I reached over his neck with my right hand and (continuing to keep the practice of kindness in the forefront of my mind) gently took the off-side rein in my hand. I did the same with my left hand on the near-side rein. As I slowly began to take up gentle contact on both reins, I could almost immediately feel the horse's mouth begin to soften. I was barely holding the reins between my fingers, but was surprised at not only how much and how willing the horse was to try to give, but also how much I was able to feel from him while he did.

The connection was so clear between the two of us that within seconds, I could literally feel the horse's entire body balanced in my hands.

"What's he doing?" the woman said, a hint of surprise in her voice.

"He's softening," I said, using the feel between the two of us to ever so subtly rock his weight back.

"No, what is he doing with his body?" She looked down at her horse. "It feels like his raising his back! He's never raised his back!"

The horse had not only softened his mouth, poll, and neck, but that same softness had very quickly traveled through his body to the point that he could engage his core, which was allowing him to lift his back and also engage his hindquarters. It felt as though the three of us were balanced on a very fine, imaginary line, similar to the feeling I used to have when I was a kid and practiced standing in the middle of a teeter-totter.

Then, I tried to get the board into perfect balance, with both ends an equal distance from the ground. I had learned, even back then, that balancing the teeter-totter in such a way was an exercise that only worked well when my body was completely soft and pliable, which then allowed it to be available to accept the movement of the board instead of fight it. That kind of availability allowed me to become part of the movement, which in turn allowed me to direct the movement. In addition, I always thought of the exercise as being fun, and there was always joy to it for me, as opposed to it being stressful and something to worry about getting right. Obviously, the stress and worry are what would have put tension in my body, which would have made the exercise much more difficult.

The same thing was happening with that horse. The intent of kindness, which automatically carried with it an element of internal as well as external softness, had been transferred through the initial contact with the reins and into the horse, creating an availability that was allowing for the type of balance the three of us were experiencing. As we stood there, it became very clear that the horse was just waiting for some direction as to what to do next. Before that feeling went away, I thought about him taking a step backward . . . and he did.

While maintaining contact with him through the reins, I asked for another step backward, and he obliged. Soon he began moving backward so smoothly that he felt as though he was floating, with almost no contact from me on the reins whatsoever.

"How did you do that?" the woman asked. "That's the farthest he's ever backed as long as I've owned him!"

To answer her question, I asked her to pick up the reins while I held the other end, between her and the horse's mouth, and showed her the feel I was using to communicate with her horse.

"My God." The look on her face was one of confusion. "There's almost nothing there! How can he feel that?"

"Horses are pretty subtle animals," I replied. "I expect he could feel much less than that, if we gave him a chance."

It was then, as she picked up the reins, that I felt what I'm sure the majority of horses are feeling when their riders pick up the reins. Even though it was obvious that she was trying to do it as softly as she could, the tension in the feel was palpable. When I tried to soften her a little more, she took the little "feel" I offered by pulling in the reins.

And that was when I began to understand the power of initial contact with softness. By making that initial contact with as much softness as possible, what happens after the contact is much easier to adjust. However, when the initial contact is made through tension, whether that tension is external, internal, or both, trying to make adjustments to develop softness becomes much more difficult, if for no other reason than the horse (and to some extent, the rider) is already on the defensive.

As when making contact in the dojo, if the initial contact is harder than is needed to influence movement, the partner being moved is bound to tighten his or her body to defend against the tension being used against them. The interesting thing here is that, while having had a conceptual understanding of this for quite some time, I had never really felt it so clearly in practice with a horse and rider as I did that day. It was one of those moments that I think everybody experiences in their lives: we know we have reached a turning point, and once the turn is made, there's no going back.

Several years have passed since that day in the dojo with my friend, and since the day with that horse and rider during that clinic. Every day, I have made a conscious effort to keep in mind the idea that softness doesn't begin after we make contact, it happens before. It happens in the intent we have within ourselves and carry in our everyday lives, and is honed in the way we practice that intent in everything we do.

I think back to how the Old Man of my childhood made his initial contact with the horses, people, and even inanimate objects that surrounded him. With hindsight, I understand that whether his actions were intentional or not, they were certainly a practice in softness, and thus, in horsemanship. Today, many years later, I, too, am making an effort to be mindful of how I make contact with things around me. In doing so, I have come to understand, perhaps, what the Old Man no doubt already knew.

True horsemanship is developed in the mindful quality of everything we do—not just in the quality of everything we do with our horses.

The Difference Between "Make" and "Help"

Walter Josey

I have been using the knowledge Mark shared with me when he stopped by on his way to a clinic he was doing in California. I'd like to share a few thoughts with you about that experience.

During that stop, Mark explained the difference in feel between the words "make" and "help" to me and a couple of friends. To illustrate the point, he used a small, thin stick about a foot-and-a-half long and about a quarter-inch in diameter. He had my two friends each hold one end of the stick, and then asked them to pull on it so the stick was being drawn with an equal amount of pressure in opposite directions (as you might do during a tug of war). He then had me take hold of the middle of the stick with one of my hands and asked me to choose a direction toward one or the other of my friends. Then he asked me to physically make the stick move in the direction I had chosen. I did, only to find the amount of pressure I needed in order to actually move the stick was way more than I had anticipated.

He then asked me to stop and try again. But this time, instead of making the stick move, say, toward the person on the right, I was to help the person on the right move the stick in that direction. I must tell you, I found that figuring out how to get the stick to move with it being held on each end was profound. I was so surprised at how that felt when I finally got it going. It didn't feel at all like I expected it would—or maybe even more important, should.

After the lesson, on the way to dinner, Mark asked me what I had learned during that experience. I was still in such a state of bewilderment that I could not give him a good answer. I had to let the lesson soak in over time.

Anyone who has searched for the magic within horses and pursued knowledge to achieve a connection between self and horse will hear about

Tom Dorrance. I, like many others, read his book looking for answers but came away more confused than ever. Some of the things he talked about seemed so mysterious yet so enticing.

One of the things that he says has stayed with me: When things are right, it feels like nothing to get your horse to work with you. This is what I felt when, focusing on the word "help," the stick started to move. It felt like nothing, yet it was doing something.

The first few times I tried to move the stick, I was using muscle. Mark saw my frustration. When I calmed my mind, thought about my center, and focused on a thought, trying to absorb the phrases Mark kept repeating— "You're doing this together," "Help the person holding the stick move in that direction," and so forth—I was finally able to get it to work.

Now here's something very interesting. As I began to walk over to the stick on my fifth attempt, I saw something that freaked me out. The stick was moving the direction I was thinking about before I even touched it. I actually saw this happening but did not know what to make of it. When I reached for the stick, it moved easily. I was both amazed and happy. Then I realized that I only had the stick cradled lightly between my forefinger and thumb, whereas before I was using my tightly curled fist, trying to muscle the stick in the direction I wanted it to go. I didn't realize I had been doing this until I released my grip.

Of course, I repeated the technique a few times to make sure I at least had a working knowledge of it. During the repetitions, it began to dawn on me how strange the whole sensation was. I can't tell you how odd it was to me; how it was so much different than the feel I was using during my earlier days of riding.

After that day, I rode my horse Scarlet actively looking for and search-ing out the "nothing feel," looking for the opportunity to do this together. It has been a fantastic experience for both of us. This may be accurate, or real, or true, or just a figment of my imagination, but my horse tells me I've stepped into a very cool realm, one that we are both having fun exploring.

My hope is that when the things I offer Scarlet feel like nothing to me, they feel the same to her. No trouble, no friction, no worry. Just open com-munication that allows us to achieve a common goal.

It was a big help to me that day to hear the feedback from the stick holders, who said they could sense the direction I was thinking about as I was about to "help" the stick move, and it was very real to them.

However, when I tried to use muscle, they felt no direction at all from me, only the strength I was using to get the stick to move, which ultimately caused both of them to resist.

I once heard Mark say, "There is a big difference between doing nothing and not doing anything." Back then, I wasn't sure I understood what he meant. But after that day of experiencing the difference between "make" and "help," I believe I do.

Friction 5

Three weeks had passed since we moved into the new, four-bedroom, two-bathroom house. It was the summer before my eighth-grade school year, and while the move had been, for me, bittersweet, I was beginning to see the benefits of the seemingly monstrous abode.

Our family of eight had come from a 900-square-foot house with only two small bedrooms and one tiny bathroom. The four of us boys shared one bedroom, our parents had the other, and my two sisters slept on a foldout couch in the living room. To say the little house was cramped was an understatement, although having grown up not knowing any different, the place had actually seemed fine to me. In truth, I just assumed all families lived in a similar way, in similar-sized houses, because all of the families on our block lived like we did. Most of the families in the neighborhood were at least as large as ours, and some were even larger. Because all of the houses in the area had been built in the early 1950s, they all looked the same, with similar floor plans and similar space restrictions.

For months leading up to the move, I had been anxious about leaving the only home and neighborhood that I'd known, the place I'd lived since I was born and the friends I'd had for as long as I could remember. I was also feeling bad about leaving the Old Man and all his horses; many was the night I lay awake trying to figure out a way to cover the fifteen-mile distance from our new house in the next town over back to his little horse ranch. Riding my bike the mile or so from the house I had grown up in to his ranch had never been much of an issue for me. But fifteen miles one-way, with part of that on a highway—now that was another story. That would have been a thirty-mile round trip, and even as naïve as I was at the time, I knew it was probably out of reach for me and my little Stingray bike. For that reason alone, I really didn't want to move.

But move we did. After three days of unpacking, with all eight of us pitching in, we not only had everything out of the boxes, but those belongings had been carefully unwrapped, and then just as carefully put into the places in the new house where, ultimately, many would remain untouched for nearly thirty years.

Once all the unpacking was finished, it was time to go out and explore the new neighborhood. I soon found it to be a friendly enough place, and I even made new friends rather quickly. However, I also noticed something about this new place that I found a little disconcerting. No matter where I went in the neighborhood, or in the town for that matter, there was an ever-present, although often sporadic, loud banging and booming sound.

Sometimes the sound would be very staccato: BOOM, BOOM, BOOM . . . BANG, BANG, BANG, BANG. Other times it would be relatively singular: BOOM. Regardless of the timing, I soon found that it went on twenty-four hours a day, seven days a week, 365 days a year.

While the noise itself was a bit unsettling, what was even more unsettling was the fact that nobody I came in contact with—adult, teenager, or child—seemed to notice or even acknowledge that the noise existed. For a while there, I felt a little like I had moved right into a real-life episode of the Twilight Zone, one where I was the only person in the world that could hear this very loud and very distinctive noise!

It would be weeks before I finally got up enough nerve to talk to one of my newfound friends, Joey Ramm, about the noise. My question came as we were walking through the small park across from his house, directly following a particularly loud BOOM, followed by an equally loud series of BANGS, one right after the other.

"What's that noise?"

"What noise?" he asked, with a look of bewilderment on his face.

BANG, BANG, BANG, BANG.

"THAT noise!" I said, incredulously.

He stopped for a minute and listened. He furrowed his brow, as if trying to hear what I was talking about but unable to.

BOOM, BOOM, BOOM . . . BANG, BANG, BANG.

"Can't you hear that?" I pointed in the direction I thought the noise was coming from. Joey looked in the direction.

BANG, BANG, BANG.

He looked back at me questioningly. "The switching?" he said, as if I should have known what he meant.

"Switching?"

"Yeah." He shrugged. "The switching."

I paused for a minute to give him time to explain, but no explanation came. "What switching?" I finally asked.

"The trains," he said flatly. "Over in the yards. I guess I don't even hear 'em anymore."

"What are they switching?"

"Cars," he said, matter-of-factly. "We have a big train yard east of town. Sometimes trains that are going one place have cars attached to them that are going somewhere else. So they unhook those cars in the yard, then a switch engine picks the cars up and puts them on a sidetrack. When all the cars that are going to the same place are all together, the train that's going to take them to wherever they're going backs into them, picks them up, and away they go."

BANG, BANG, BANG, BANG.

"That's just the sound of the cars coupling," he said. "You wanna go see? It's not far."

"Sure," I said, interested in actually seeing what had been the cause of so much of my anxiety over the past several weeks. Without saying another word, Joey turned toward the sound and started walking. I went with him.

The neighborhood our family had just moved into was very new, and the neighborhood that Joey's house was in was fairly new, but as we left the park heading east, we immediately entered an obviously older area. The houses there were tall and narrow, many of them were run-down, and they all seemed to have been built only a few feet from one another. Some of the houses had four-foot chain-link fences around the little grassy area in front of them, and many had dogs of various sizes running loose inside the fence that ran at the fence and barked ferociously as we walked by.

Joey, unfazed, walked past them as if they weren't there. As we continued on our way, meandering through one old neighborhood after another, Joey gave me the history of the little town. It had been a railroad hub for longer than anybody could remember. Not for passenger trains, but for freight trains. Because it was roughly halfway between the northern and southern part of the state, it was a perfect spot for shippers to drop their freight so it could be moved in either direction. While many trains simply passed through the hub, many more stopped long enough to drop cars that would later be picked up by another train and moved to their final southern or northern destination.

After leaving the last of the old neighborhoods, we stepped into a small corner grocery store with a hardwood floor and an old man in a white shirt, tie, and grocer's apron sitting behind the counter. A little bell above the door rang as we passed through, and the grocer smiled at us as we entered. Joey and I each bought five pieces of Bazooka Joe bubble gum, then continued on our way. We walked past the Iron Horse Tavern, then the Side Track Inn, both pretty seedy old bars that reeked of stale whisky and cigarette smoke, even though their front doors were closed at the time. And then, a little past the bars, we came on a small, grassy field, and beyond that, a sharp rise that led up to the rail yards.

Just below the rise was a pit filled with stagnant water and lined with beer bottles and trash. Joey called that area the "steam pit," and said that in the old days, it was where the old steam engines would dump the water from their boilers before they went in for repairs. Since that time, however, it had become little more than an area where rainwater collected, and it had also become a gathering place where high school kids hung out and drank beer. My initial thought, as we passed by, was that a less attractive place for such an activity would have been pretty hard to find.

After passing the steam pit, we climbed the rise that led to the rail yards. As we did, I had no way of knowing that what I was about to see would ultimately have a positive impact on my horsemanship in years to come.

Not more than about forty feet from the crest of the rise were three separate sidetracks, each with train cars sitting on them. Almost as soon as we got to the top of the rise, a switch engine (a locomotive considerably smaller than a "road locomotive," used for disassembling and reassembling trains) slid slowly on to one of the sidetracks and thumped into one of the cars that was waiting there. There was a very loud BOOM as couplers engaged; it literally shook the ground. The railroad car that had been sitting on the track jerked backward when the switcher hit it. After coupling, the engine reversed direction and the car jerked forward with a very loud BANG.

The switch engine moved a way down the track, past an intersection where a man on the ground threw a switch that allowed the intersecting track to slide over. Once the track was in place, the switch engine reversed direction, again, creating another loud BANG as the car it was attached to began moving. The pair rolled back down the line and onto another sidetrack, where they collided with the set of cars on that track. BOOM, BANG, BANG, BANG, BANG. The noise was deafening as the cars slid into one another.

After all the cars had been coupled, the switch engine pulled forward once again, taking the string of cars with it. BANG, BANG, BANG, and BANG—the cars all jumped into line. The small locomotive then took the entire string of cars off the sidetrack and rolled them down the main track, around a corner, and out of sight.

Joey and I stayed a little longer, then retraced our steps to our own neighborhood. I must say, I felt much better after our visit to the yard, what with the mystery of the strange sounds having been solved and all. In fact, it wasn't long before all that banging and booming from the train yards just seemed to disappear from my consciousness. When someone who had come to visit would ask me, "What's that noise?" I, too, found myself answering, "What noise?"

Now I'm sure many folks just read this little story and are wondering what the heck any of it has to do with the concept of softness, or even anything that might even remotely have to do with horses, for that matter. The answer is simple. There was a principle at work that day that many horse people unwittingly use, often to their disadvantage, on a regular basis when working with their horses: static friction.

Basically, the idea behind static friction is that if we abruptly push or pull on something when it is stationary, the thing that is stationary will get stuck, or appear to be heavier than it really is. However, if enough force and/ or mass is applied during the initial contact between the moving object and the stationary one, the stationary object will break free, although usually with some kind of major turmoil.

In the case of the train cars Joey and I had been watching, the switch engine collided with a stationary car. This collision in turn caused the car it ran into to become momentarily stuck to the track. But because there was so much force, energy, and mass behind the engine, the car had no choice but to break loose and move. However, instead of the car's movement being smooth and effortless, it lurched violently in the direction the engine was pushing (or pulling), in turn creating a thunder-like sound that could be heard for miles in every direction.

Now, this principle occurs quite frequently in horsemanship. Because few of us know or understand it, we often end up repeating the same "abrupt" behaviors with our horses over and over, and continue to get the same unfortunate results. For instance, it is not uncommon to see a rider whose horse spooks or jumps unexpectedly brusquely snatch a rein in order to get the horse under control or give it direction.

Almost always when the rider uses that kind of force and energy, the horse has no alternative but to lock its jaw and stiffen its neck. A horse does this partially out of self-defense, and partially because the abruptness of the movement automatically creates the same kind of static friction in the horse's body that was caused when the switch engine crashed into those boxcars. In other words, physics dictates that the horse's body responds to the abruptness of the contact by first getting stuck. Only after that (and assuming enough force had been applied during contact in the first place) will the horse's body actually break loose and move in the direction that was demanded by the rider. But even then, the horse is seldom moving willingly or softly.

The effects of static friction can also be seen when a rider abruptly uses his or her legs on a horse's sides, as in when a horse is kicked or spurred. The horse's body will jerk at the moment of impact, or perhaps it will give a head toss or tail swish, or a combination of all three, before it actually begins moving. The same can be said for how a horse responds when a lead rope attached to a halter is jerked or shaken by a handler. In each of these cases, the horse will almost always become "stuck" before the desired movement comes through; even then, the movement that does come through is almost always awkward and faltering.

In contrast, there is another, much more beneficial principle that can be used in horsemanship that has almost the complete opposite effect on the horse when used properly: dynamic friction. Whereas static friction relies primarily on force, mass, and energy to first stick an object before moving it, dynamic friction relies on establishing subtle movement first, then adding energy to build on that movement.

The example I always use when explaining this idea to riders is this: Let's say our car has broken down on the side of the road and a friend pulls up and offers to use his car to push the stalled one home. At that point, we have a couple of options. Our friend can back up, get his vehicle up to thirty or forty miles per hour, and then crash into the back of the stalled car, thus establishing movement. Or, he could ease his car up to the back of the stalled one, ever-so-gently move up against the bumper, and then begin to slowly push the stalled car forward.

During the first example (static friction), the stalled vehicle would undoubtedly move, but not before first getting stuck upon impact and con-sequently causing quite a bit of damage to both vehicles in the process. In the second example (dynamic friction), movement is easily established and then built upon with little or no damage to either vehicle. In fact, within a very short period of time after establishing that initial subtle contact and movement, both vehicles could easily be moving forty, fifty, or sixty miles an hour, without damage to either.

This is the idea behind dynamic friction: establish subtle movement in a stationary object prior to trying to develop bigger movement. The appli-cation of this idea in horsemanship is to establish contact with the horse, followed by the development of subtle movement to establish a flow of direction, and finally putting the proper amount of speed into that flow so as to accomplish the desired task.

I bring up these two principles involving friction and relate them to horsemanship because when we are talking about developing softness, it's important to know how the mechanics of what we do can effect the out-come of our request. You see, a number of years ago when I first went out on the road doing clinics, I was taken back by the abruptness with which some riders used their reins. Some of this was due to the fact that a few riders were just trying to get the correct timing on their requests, and in doing so, were hurrying more than they needed to. But I was also seeing a great number of riders who had taken to discarding contact with their horse through the reins, and thus riding with a great deal of slack between their hands and their horse's mouth.

In and of itself, riding with a lot of slack in the reins is not a bad thing, especially if the horse is far enough along in its training to be able to respond softly to a request from the rider's hands. Unfortunately, however, that wasn't usually what I was seeing. Many of the riders I was working with at the time had, in effect, thrown their reins away because they had either been taught that was how they were supposed to ride, or had been told by an instructor, trainer, or clinician that their hands weren't skilled enough to be able to ride with a shorter rein.

In the meantime, because the rider had avoided, and in some cases, abandoned, rein contact with the horse, neither the horse nor the rider developed the skills needed to either use or respond to contact. What was happening instead was that riders were on horses who didn't understand how to stop, turn, back up, and, in some cases, even walk a straight line, and horses had riders on their backs who didn't really understand how to request those things in the first place.

As a result, any time one of these riders wanted to ask something of the horse, such as a simple turn, the rider would first have to gather up all that sagging rein, which in some cases amounted to literally two or three feet of slack, before even making contact with the bit! The problem was that usually by the time the rider finally made contact with the bit, there was so much momentum built up that he or she would end up banging the bit with considerable force, causing the horse to lock its jaw and stiffen its neck. This, in turn, gave the impression that the horse was hard-mouthed, ignorant, or just plain contrary. In reality, it was physics and self-defense that actually dictated the horse's response.

In most cases, the folks who were riding in such a way had no idea that they were the cause of the problem they were having with their horse. One such rider was a woman in England who we were working with. She rode a big bay gelding that seemed on edge even before she brought him into the arena. As she tried in vain to ride a circle around me, she explained that she was having a difficult time getting her horse to walk a straight line and stop, and when I asked how well he backed up, she replied, "He doesn't."

She continued to ride the shapeless circle while at the same time explaining that she had been spending quite a bit of time working on developing "lightness" in her hands. As a result, she was very proud to report that she was able to use almost no pressure whatsoever with the reins. Of course, she was completely oblivious to the fact that her horse was really struggling with the lack of direction he was getting, and because of that, was doing little more than nervously wandering in the general direction she seemed to want him to go.

About that same time, her horse turned off the circle she was trying to keep him on and very deliberately walked straight over to the gate. As he did, the woman tried to snatch the slack from the left rein in an attempt to turn him back into the middle of the arena where I was standing. It took a couple of seconds for her to actually make contact, and by the time she did, she had put a considerable amount of force into the effort she was using. Of course, her horse stiffened and continued on his way toward the gate, which in turn caused her to use even more pressure on the bit, which in turn cause the horse to stiffen more.

In no time at all, the horse was standing with his head over the gate. His rider, rein in hand and arm extended way over her head in an attempt to keep the slack from the rein and maintain contact with him, tried to explain to me how belligerent he was being.

I walked over, gently took the rein the woman was holding, and turned her and the horse away from the gate, leading them part way back to the center of the arena. As I turned them loose, the horse almost immediately turned back toward the gate. The woman, attempting to take up the slack from the rein once again, very quickly extended her arm above her head, banging the horse in the mouth. The horse stiffened and continued on his way.

I walked after them, caught and turned the horse, and led them both back all the way to the center of the arena. There I stopped them so that I could talk with the rider.

"A minute ago," I started, "you mentioned that you don't have to use much pressure with the reins to get the horse to respond."

"That's right," she nodded.

"But you were using quite a bit just then, and he wasn't responding."

"I wasn't using very much, actually," she smiled.

"On a scale from zero to ten with zero being no pressure and ten being way more than you would want to use," I asked as I lightly stroked the gelding on his head, "how much would you say you had in the rein just then?"

"Not very much," she repeated.

"On a scale from zero to ten?"

She hesitated for a second or two, her eyes drifting upward in thought. "A five, or perhaps six?" She posed it as a question rather than a statement.

"I would agree with that," I nodded. "So we were using a five or a six on that pressure scale and he wasn't responding?"

"Yes, I suppose that's right."

"And how much pressure would you like to be using, on that scale?"

"As little as possible," she replied. "A one or two."

"Well, then," I smiled. "Let's see if we can teach him how to respond consistently to a one or two."

I went on to explain that riding that particular horse with that much slack in the reins was causing a couple of problems for the two of them. The first was she didn't seem to have much control over what her horse did, which was evident by the fact he couldn't stay on the circle she had put him on, he couldn't walk a straight line when she asked him to, and he couldn't stop upon request. The second was that when she did need to say something to him through the use of the reins, she had to first get so much slack out of them that by the time she actually made contact, too much time passed. Not only was her timing off, she also couldn't help but hit him in the mouth with the bit due to the momentum in her arm, which in turn caused him to brace, and her to pull.

To help change things up a little between the two of them, I spent some time adjusting her reins and removing the majority of the slack. Then we worked with her hands; I showed her how to use pressure with the reins without pulling. Finally, I showed her how to use the movement in her hands in such a way that she wasn't inadvertently causing her horse to lock his jaw and stiffen his neck.

Within just a few minutes of making the adjustments, she and her horse were not only able to walk a straight line, but they could also ride a nice round circle as well. Not long after that, their stops began to improve, and the two of them even began backing up fairly nicely, with the rider using almost exactly the amount of pressure she had wanted to use in the first place.

Now, the reason I mention this particular horse and rider is that they very clearly illustrate the kind of changes that can occur when we go from creating static friction to dynamic friction. Her horse didn't want to be acting the way he was, but he had no choice. In her attempt to have "light" hands, she had actually become ineffective in her communication. And then when she really did need to communicate with him—when he started heading for the gate, for instance—she ended up using way more pressure than she needed. By making contact so abruptly, she was causing him to get "stuck," which in turn caused her to pull on the bit and him to push against the pull.

I often liken this abruptness to using our arms and hands as if they are being driven by pistons. As most folks know, the movement of a piston is fairly curt. It quickly pops one way, and then it quickly pops the other. Again, it is this abruptness of movement that tends to create the static friction that often gets our horses stuck and/or resistant.

In contrast, when trying to develop dynamic friction, the movement in our hands and arms is smooth and flowing, as if being driven by hydraulics. It is this smoothness of movement that allows us to make a soft initial contact, which then almost always allows for the creation of willing movement in the direction we want, without a brace in our horse.

While it is a very good thing to understand how easy it is to either create static friction or dynamic friction in our horse just by the way we use our reins, there is another, even more beneficial type of friction that we can generate through the way we handle them to which we seldom, if ever give any thought. This third idea is known as kinetic friction and using it can often defuse certain seemingly dangerous situations without anybody getting hurt and without making the situation worse than it already is.

The principle behind kinetic friction is simple. Basically, a mass that is moving can be brought to a stop by providing some sort of drag, or opposing force, to that moving mass. Kinetic friction is what stops glaciers from traveling indefinitely. It's what stops a soccer ball from rolling into the next county after it's been kicked, and it's what can help a panicky horse stop fighting someone who is holding the other end of its lead rope.

Many years ago, this principle accidentally became very clear to me while helping a friend move his horses from winter pasture back to his ranch. After gathering many of the horses off the 2,500-acre pasture and putting them in a nearby catch pen, he took note of which horses we had caught, then decided which, out of the seventy-five or so we had gathered, he would be taking to the ranch.

After selecting eight-head, he and I haltered and then led them to the trailer. We tied them to a nearby hitch rail, and he asked me to start loading what we had while he went back and got two more. I agreed, and as he returned to the catch pen, I began taking the horses, two at a time from the hitch rail and loading them into the first compartment of the ten-horse stock trailer. Once in the trailer, I tied one horse to the right side so it would be facing right, and the other to the left side, facing left. The horses were then basically standing nose to tail.

I got the first four loaded without incident and brought the fifth and sixth horses from the hitch rail to the trailer. One was a fifteen-hand bay gelding, the other a very sweet-looking dun mare who couldn't have been more than fourteen hands, with big round eyes, a delicate and refined face and features, and a long black mane and tail. I tied the gelding to the right side of the trailer; then, as I began to bring the mare close enough to other side of the trailer to tie her, she suddenly and violently pulled back.

She scrambled backward in a panic, but because I had her lead rope draped over the crook of my arm as I brought her in, she felt no tension on the rope as she pulled back. I wasn't fast enough to actually take hold of the rope as it zinged across the crook of my arm during her departure, so I just tried to move with her instead as she backed away. She landed flat-footed on the ground outside the trailer and then just stood, shaking her head as if the whole thing was quite a surprise to her.

I gave her a second to catch her breath, then gently took the lead rope and brought her back inside the trailer. Again, just as I got to where I could tie her off, she blew backward. I was ready for her this time, and having seen how vehement she was about getting out, knew better than to clamp my hand around the rope. Had I done that she would have just had something to pull against, which would have made her stronger, and no doubt would have given me a first-class rope burn in the process. So, with my hand loosely holding the rope, I again moved with her as she took herself out of the trailer.

Oddly enough, this second time, she didn't seem to be nearly as worried about the whole thing, and in fact, only used about half the energy she had during her first escape. After she got out, I let her settle for a couple of minutes, then brought her back in the trailer. She took herself out of the trailer twice more, each time cutting the energy she used to get out in half, until finally I was able to walk her in and have her stand quietly. Once it was clear she was comfortable standing next to the gelding, I tied her off and closed the divider to the compartment she was in. I had just loaded the remaining two horses as my friend walked up, leading the last two from the catch pen.

"Where's Lady?" he asked, a bit perplexed.

"Which one is Lady?"

"The little dun mare that was tied over there." He pointed to the spot on the hitch rail where the little mare that had trouble loading had been tied.

"She's in the middle, next to that red gelding," I said, pointing to where she was tied inside the trailer.

He walked over to the side of the trailer and looked in at the mare standing quietly.

"How'd you get her all the way in there?" He seemed a bit surprised.

"Just led her in a couple times," I said, shrugging my shoulders.

"Did she put up a fight?"

"Not really." I replied. "She backed out a few times, but other than that she wasn't any trouble. Why?"

"I forgot to warn you about her. She'll take your arm off pulling back when you go to load her, if you're not careful. We gave up on loading her that far in. We usually just put her on the very back and don't tie her." He took another look at her. "How'd you get her in there, again?"

Of course, I didn't really know it at the time, but what I had actually done was create kinetic friction between the mare and myself. That is, I used just enough drag on the rope for the mare to feel a little resistance, but not so much that she felt like she wanted to fight more than she already was. What she probably felt was something close to what she might have experienced had there been only the natural resistance of her own movement.

Here's another way to look at it. If we kick a soccer ball one time and it rolls across the ground, the simple friction of the ball's surface against the surface of the grass, coupled with the resistance of the earth's atmosphere, will eventually bring the ball to a stop. All of those forces together will just naturally stop the ball from moving.

The same goes for a moving horse (or anything else, for that matter). Even when a horse panics, all of those forces are still at work, and regardless of how scary the situation, eventually the horse will stop moving. To help in situations like that, if we can find a way to add just slightly to those forces, either through guiding with the lead rope or rein, without actually crossing over into static friction, we can usually help the horse give in a little more quickly. But if we add to the energy the horse is already using by fighting with it (or, in this case, had I tried to demand that the mare stay in the trailer by clamping down on the lead rope), it will surely take much longer for the horse to calm down and slow to a stop.

As I mentioned at the outset, these three principles—static friction, dynamic friction, and kinetic friction—are things we rarely think about when working with our horses. When it comes to training, we usually look at things in terms of the horse's behavior, and whether or not the behavior we're getting is the behavior we're looking for. If the behavior isn't what we want, and we're conscientious about our work, we usually try to figure out what's causing the problem. But even then, we don't often look to ourselves as the possible originator of the issues.

In other words, if our horse is bracing against the bit (for instance), we often just assume he is a "bracey" or hard-mouthed horse, and work backward from there—meaning we do things to try to soften the brace after it is already present. We seldom give any thought to the fact that the speed or abruptness with which we pick up the reins might actually be causing the brace. We also don't give much thought to trying to change the way we make initial contact as a way to create softness and/or movement so that the horse does not feel that he has to brace or defend himself in the first place.

By also taking time to understand the effects these three distinct principles have during the handling of our horses, we might then be able to see that there is actually a very broad range of possibilities available to us, not only as far as solutions go, but also as far as potential causes.

And in the end, the broader our spectrum of knowledge, the easier it is for us to find effective ways of communicating. The better our communication, the more paths we'll see to the development of true softness—in ourselves, and our horses.

The More You Listen, the More You Hear

Lee Cranney

People often ask me how long I've been flying, and my usual response is, "All my life." But I actually started flight school in 1967, so it's really only been 47 or so years. In my long and somewhat checkered career, I've flown slicks and gunship helicopters, jets and turboprop airplanes. I've carried VIPs and troops, dynamite, cargo, and chickens and pigs, and fought fires and bad guys. I've flown on instruments without reference to the ground, relying on radar and radio navigation aids.

Today, I fly the Sikorsky Firehawk helicopter for the Los Angeles County Fire Department. We fight wildland fires; rescue lost hikers, climbers, and the occasional horse; and fly patients from accident scenes to hospitals. Even after almost five decades, I continue to enjoy every minute of it. As we fortunate few who get to do what we love are fond of saying, "It sure beats working for a living."

I have been hanging out with horses for less than a quarter of the time I've been flying, and most of that has been with my buddy, Dude, but I have loved every single second of it. If you had suggested to me ten years ago that I would fall in love with a horse, let alone horses plural, I likely would have said you were nuts. When Dude was offered to me free of charge as a two-year-old, I was told that he had "issues." My first question was, "What's an issue?" Today, I would take a bullet for him, and I think he knows it.

If Dude could, he'd tell you, "My human is a slow learner . . . but I try hard to be patient with him." His relief when I finally started to "get" how to sit the trot was palpable. I have been told by more than one person that almost anybody else would have "sent that horse down the road" a long time ago. And maybe I should have. Let's just say that Dude and I have proven the axiom that "green horse plus green rider equals black-and-blue."

Anyway, when Mark asked if I would share my ideas on how flying helicopters might relate to softness and feel with horses, my first reaction was, "Huh?"

But as I thought about it, I began to realize that a lot of what I have spent my life learning does actually apply in many ways to getting along with horses. I would like to share some of that with you. Allow me to set the stage with a little bit about the basics of flying helicopters.

Let's start with a short comparison between airplanes and airplane pilots, and helicopters and their pilots. It has been truly said that airplanes are fundamentally stable and want to fly. If left alone, they will motor along nicely, sometimes for hours if trimmed up properly. And if something does go wrong, they glide with a pretty sedate rate of descent that gives their pilots a lot of time to sort out the problem and what they want to do about. Not always, of course (the "Hudson River landing" for example), but usually.

Airplane pilots, as a result, tend to be optimists.

Helicopters—aptly described as "a million moving parts flying in close formation"—by their very nature are inherently unstable and very much do not want to fly. If left to their own devices once in flight, and absent a very expensive multi-axis autopilot, they will immediately "turn turtle" and head for the ground in an uncontrollable descent.

Helicopter pilots, then, tend to be devout pessimists, constantly running through their minds what to do in the event any of the rotating parts (engines, blades, rotors, and so forth) decide to diverge from the aforementioned very tight "formation" parameters set up so the thing will actually fly. Constantly checking and rechecking (literally with all five senses) for something amiss in any of the myriad systems (drive train, rotor system, hydraulics, avionics, electrical) all while keeping the thing purring along to its next destination.

In my opinion, really good helicopter pilots spend their flying time secure in the knowledge that they can handle whatever is about to go wrong. I believe the same can be said of really good horsemen (not that I am or likely ever will be one). Constantly feeling the whole horse, constantly aware of what holds his attention, intention, and thoughts, his movements, feet, weight, and balance, secure in the knowledge they can handle whatever is about to go wrong.

The similarities between flying helicopters and working with horses are both more basic and much more complex. Helicopters, like all aircraft, have a design gross operating weight that depends on several flight weather conditions, including altitude, temperature, and wind.

From day one of flight school, helicopter pilots have instilled in them the concepts of control touch and pilot technique. These two concepts are, in practice, identical to softness and feel; if I move the cyclic control (the "joy stick" or simply the "stick") a minutely small amount, the commensurate effect on the main rotor is significantly more. This gives the helicopter amazing maneuverability and versatility but makes it extremely touchy ("squirrelly," if you will). Experienced pilots will typically rest their right hands on their right thighs and make small, almost imperceptible inputs to the cyclic to achieve desired changes (sounds somewhat like horsemanship, don't you think?). And, just to make it a little more interesting, any input in any one of the five controls requires a compensating corrective or offsetting control input in all of the others: "Rub your belly, pat your head."

To illustrate: an average pilot can take off from a hover with the aircraft at the design gross weight for that altitude, temperature, and wind condition. If he ham-fists or over-controls during the maneuver, the aircraft will actually settle back to the ground rather than take off. Normally (and if the pilot in command has ensured that the aircraft is loaded for the conditions), there is a built-in "fudge factor" of power available to compensate and still allow an average pilot to make the takeoff. A pilot who cultivates control touch (softness) and pilot technique (feel) can, in fact, get the same aircraft off the ground smoothly and with less power. Inevitably, in the life of a working helicopter pilot, there will come a time when he needs that control touch and pilot technique to save the aircraft and all on board. Consequently, softness and feel are drummed into us as the way to get the most from our machines in the worst conditions.

I remember spending some time with another clinician several years ago and hearing him say, "Now, ask your horse for that soft feel." While

I totally understood the idea (pilot technique), I had no clue how to ask Dude for it or how to recognize whether or not he had answered.

Enter Mark Rashid. At our first clinic together, Mark spent a goodly amount of time (remember, I'm a pretty slow learner) showing us both what a soft feel looked and felt like, as well as how to ask for it and how to recognize the answer.

In subsequent clinics, we built on that knowledge. Imagine my astonishment when much, much later, I began to experience the effortless beauty of asking for a soft feel, or change of gait, or turn with no touch at all; simply thought, connection, and breath and then we do it. Together. As one. Doesn't happen all the time, of course, but when it does, it is truly amazing. And almost enough to make a grown man bawl. So, softness and feel equate to pilot technique and control touch. Okay. Makes some sense.

Now, I realize that Dude and I are blessed with no ticking clocks, no cattle to bring in, and no real job to get done. My only job is to build the absolute best relationship possible with a horse who was very badly mishandled "on the start" and especially his first thirty days of training. (Which I have come to believe is an oxymoron. Thirty days? Really?) Hell, I recently spent months, literally, "restarting" him when I finally realized (slow study thing again) that deeply instilled within him by his "starters" was the idea that tacking up was going to lead to some fearful, perhaps painful, stuff. Carrying that bottled anxiety throughout each and every ride made him spring-loaded, ready to run for cover at the first sign of something he was unsure of.

Then there's this: One day while I was on Dude, Mark said that I should "ride the whole horse." I got the concept immediately. Remember earlier when I mentioned using all five senses to fly the aircraft? (If you wonder about using taste and smell to fly, I'd be happy to explain it to you, but it gets a little overlong.) I was able to translate that awareness of the whole aircraft to a slowly blossoming awareness of the whole horse. Each foot, which way his thoughts, energy, and weight are inclined to go next. To the degree that I can stay aware of it all, I am able to stay ahead of the horse/aircraft. Pilots whose attention stays inside the cockpit tend to be unaware of situations developing around them—weather, other aircraft, fire patterns, and so forth—which sometimes results in disaster. We refer to this as situational awareness (being aware of all around us, both near and far), and it is certainly applicable to horsemanship.

I am beginning to comprehend, and to some degree, practice what Mark describes as a need to live my daily life with softness and a welcoming, blending openness if I want to apply it to my horses and horsemanship. I can't run around all day gnashing my teeth and losing my temper and then go out to spend time with Dude and be soft for him.

This is critically important these days, as Dude and I are experimenting with liberty work. It is more rewarding than I am able to share to be able to let him out of his pasture, give him free run of our ten acres, walk up to him, scratch his belly or halter him, or ask him from across the property to get out of the hay barn and have him do it. Sometimes.

But I am learning that the instant I even allow myself to be irritated or frustrated, he senses it, and whatever we were (I was) working on is doomed from that moment. So whatever he does (especially if it is not what I think I am asking him to do) becomes exactly what I was asking him to do (or at least a much better idea than mine) so that he remains open to what I was really asking him to do. If that makes sense to you, good luck—talk about walking a razor's edge.

Now, don't misunderstand; Dude is no Trigger and I am in no way Roy Rogers. (And who wants to be, right? How many horses do you think they went through before they found a Trigger that stood still for Roy when he jumped on his back from a second-story balcony? And what kind of shape was Roy in by then? Never mind—I'm digressing.) But (and I know people frown on treats for horses) Dude can hear the rustle of a sugar-free peppermint candy wrapper from across the property. Sometimes that, and my, "C'mere, Dude!" filter onto his shortlist of things he wants to do in this moment! And lo and behold, he will walk over and deign to take the candy.

Or to be able to ask him, while he is head down in the feed bin (and I'm ten feet away) to back up a half step, and have him do it. To be fair to him, though, I try to let there be a reason for my requests (belly scratch, foot check, or fly spray, for instance) but sometimes it is just because I need him to do it. And I try to let him vote when I can.

You see, I have come to believe that this whole communication thing is a two-way street. And that most horses just get used to not expecting the human to understand horse. Some time ago, when that awareness began to creep in, it seemed to me that I was obligated to really watch for anything from him that was a request or a statement. This started when (trying to follow Tom Dorrance's advice to do everything I could to help the horse want to be with me) I realized that my horses would come to me for a belly scratch from clear across the pasture; the mare will actually lift her hind leg to show me where she would like to be scratched. Huh, I thought. I wonder what else they can try to tell me they would like.

So I encourage that whenever I can. Even if they aren't trying to tell me something, I act as if they are, and lo and behold, the horse begins to realize that I am listening to him, and it begins to grow. Starts with an understanding that they can come to me for comfort (like that belly scratch, or a face rub after taking off the headstall) and who knows where it will end.

I will share a couple of recent events that no doubt fall into the "you will see it when you believe it" category. One hot morning, I drove the hay cart down to Dude and Gypsy's pasture, and they met me at the gate (some fifty feet from where I parked the cart). Gypsy, the mare, was first in line, so I started to give her a good scratching. Dude (who loves being scratched) waited patiently until I was finished. When I was done with Gypsy, I asked her to move so Dude could have a turn. She did, and as I began to walk the couple of steps to Dude, he looked me straight in the eye, turned smartly away, walked briskly to the end of the pasture where the hay cart was, stopped, and looked back at me with serious intent. "Okay, buddy," I said, "I'll get you something to eat." Wasn't lunch time but I got them all a little snack anyway. See, even if he wasn't telling me he wanted to eat (he was, but to make the point) I act "as if" and eventually, they begin to get that they have a vote.

That afternoon, while Mark was teaching, I eased myself into the arena, reached over the dividing fence to pet Dude, touched the hot wire (I forgot it was still live on that end of his pasture), and did a double back flip when the snap bit me. Every horse and human within sight or sound reacted, of course (some more athletically than others).

I sheepishly crept out of the arena, apologizing all the way.

The next morning, I was back in Dude's pasture, at the other end (where the hot wire was dead but still up). Dude, Gypsy, and I were watching Mark and his student in the arena and I realized Dude giving me an intent look.

Directing my attention to him, I asked, "What, son?" He turned deliberately to the hot wire (that was not hot) and "twanged" it with his nose. I thought, Well, that's pretty stupid for a smart horse, as he looked me right in the eye (Pay attention! he seemed to be saying) and did it again!

Either he's telling me I don't need to worry about this one or I should take it down, or both, I thought. I walked out of the pasture, went to the barn for a pair of wire cutters, came back, and took the 100-foot wire down. As I rolled it up, Dude walked away and went back to eating and I left the pasture in awe of what had just happened.

I apologize if this kind of relationship-building digresses from the topic of softness and feel (which is, of course, also relationship-building), but it is so cool that I wanted to share it. I think it's fine if you don't want to spend the time to explore this kind of stuff with your horse. But in my case, the trust that it continues to build really helps Dude feel good about himself and his lot in life, and to relax and enjoy packing me about. If I am doing something with him on the ground that worries him, he will press his nose into my sternum and look me right in the eye. I clearly understand that he wants me to reassure him that he is "all right" and that what we are doing is necessary.

It is clear to me, then, that pilot technique and control touch, staying ahead of the aircraft, and flying the whole machine are as applicable to horsemanship as they are to flying helicopters. Having them instilled in me for forty-plus years certainly doesn't make me a horseman, but I am now, thanks to Mark, able to understand softness and feel, and riding the whole horse. Sometimes I can even get them working for us.

I would like to close with a heartfelt thank you to Mark and Crissi for showing Dude and me the way. It could take a lot of words to explain how troubled Dude really was when we started working with Mark. Not too many months ago, Mark said to me, "I think you have turned the corner with this guy," and I was so grateful. It just continues to get better every ride.

So if you haven't ridden with Mark, you and your horse are missing an opportunity to experience a whole new dimension in horsemanship. No sticks, tack, or courses to buy. Just honest, expert, one-on-one ideas and suggestions to help you—and by default—your horse.

One last thought: Federal aviation regulations require pilots to perform a thorough preflight inspection. This is a fine habit we all strive to cultivate and, it seems to me, a good one for horsemen and -women as well.

So keep the pointy end forward and the dirty side down, keep the rotor in the green, and scratch his belly once in awhile. Oh, and try to let him vote on occasion.

I sincerely hope that God blesses you . . . and the horse you rode in on!

Working the Edge 6

There are a few benefits to spending as much time on the road as I do. One of them is that the view from my office window—the windshield of my truck—changes every mile or so. That may be something few folks other than professional truckers, touring musicians, and horsemanship clinicians can say.

Another great benefit is that I have an opportunity to read an awful lot of clever bumper stickers. Not only are some of these stickers fun to read, but they can be educational, too. A couple of my favorites are: "There are three kinds of people, those who can count and those who can't." And "Don't believe everything you think." I saw this one on the back of a semi tractor-trailer rig at a truck stop near Macon, Georgia: "Load it like a boxcar, drive it like a NASCAR." And one of my all-time favorites, "If you're living on the edge, you're taking up too much room."

I saw this last one on the back of an old Land Cruiser heading into the Eisenhower Tunnel here in Colorado last March as I was driving to California for a series of clinics. The vehicle was loaded down with young men and snowboards, apparently on their way to one of the many mountain ski areas. I could just picture those guys up on the slopes, years of experience already under their young belts, expertly shredding powder as if it were nothing. I suppose it is that kind of confidence of experience that allows them to proclaim, "If you're living on the edge, you're taking up too much room."

At the risk of sounding like I'm overanalyzing a bumper sticker, of all things, I find the inference of this particular saying pretty interesting. What I mean by that is, for people to "live on the edge," they must already be fairly accomplished, otherwise they wouldn't be able to get to the "edge" of their ability and still be performing in a skillful manner. So for someone to say that living on the edge is taking up "too much room," the implication is that the person making the statement is actually way beyond the level of knowledge and skill of the person who is "living on the edge."

What has this got to do with horsemanship, or softness, or anything else, for that matter, you might be asking yourself. Well, some time back, I became fascinated with a Japanese term referred to as kami-shitoe. The term itself is used to describe the space between life and death. Usually, the term is demonstrated with a sheet of very thin paper. On one side of the paper is the symbol for life, and on the other side is the symbol for death. The space between the two symbols—the thickness of the paper—represents how slight the distance between the two worlds is. In other words, we are always walking a very fine line between life and death, and often we aren't even aware of it.

But the thing that really intrigues me about this concept is that kami-shitoe can be found in everything we do. Specifically, when it comes to horsemanship, kami-shitoe can be the difference between getting something right and having it all go wrong. It could mean the difference between staying on the horse's back or falling off, it could be the difference between understanding and misunderstanding, and it could be the difference between feeling something the horse is offering or feeling nothing at all.

I suppose the first time I became aware of this very fine line was when I was a kid trying to balance in the middle of that teeter-totter. Anybody who has ever tried standing in the middle of a teeter-totter knows that once the board is in balance, it takes very little to keep it there. However, the more the board goes out of balance, the more effort it takes both to get it back in balance and to keep it in balance.

Years later, after seeing a teeter bridge designed for horses, I began playing with this exact same concept of balancing the teeter-totter with my horses. A teeter bridge is basically a platform made of wood, anywhere from three to five feet wide and up to ten feet or so long. Under the platform, about an equal distance from each end, is a small log the same width as the platform. The log serves as the board's pivot point. The idea behind the teeter bridge is that when you walk your horse over the platform, starting at one end and moving to the other, the platform tips, just as the teeter-totter would.

Keep in mind that for a very long time and prior to being asked to go out and give clinics, I had been fairly isolated as a horseman. I had worked on various high-country ranches for most of my adult life, and wasn't terribly familiar with what was going on in the "outside" training world. Because of that, I only discovered the teeter bridge after I began traveling the country doing clinics. I must admit, the first time I saw one of these bridges, I couldn't really see the practical application. After all, if I came across an unstable bridge out in the middle of nowhere, I'd more than likely go around it rather than over it. So at first I struggled a little bit to find a reason to teach my horse to go over it.

But then, as time went on, I began to see that teaching a horse to do something out of the ordinary, such as crossing that kind of bridge, might not be such a bad thing after all. Not only could it get the horse used to handling uneven ground and unexpected movement, but it could also end up being a great confidence-builder. I soon began to show my horses how to navigate these types of bridges whenever we were in a venue where they had one.

I quickly found that the horses I was traveling with and using as my clinic horses—horses I had usually raised, started, and trained—seemed completely unfazed by these obstacles. With very little coaxing, each one would look inquisitively at the bridge, paw at it a couple of times, and then step up on it like they'd been doing it all their lives. After that, getting them to walk across a teeter bridge was relatively easy and usually without incident.

Then, one day, I happened to be riding my horse Smokey while coaching a rider during a clinic. In the corner of the arena was one of these teeter bridges; after finishing the rider's session, and as we broke for lunch, Smokey and I eased ourselves over to the bridge and walked across it a time or two.

Smokey was an extremely inquisitive horse, almost to a fault, and so doing things like walking over a moving bridge were right up his alley. After the second time we went over the bridge, I asked him to step up on the bridge with just his front feet, which he did. Then, with his front feet on the bridge, I asked him to do a turn on the forehand so that his body was off to the side of the bridge while his front feet were still on it. Then, just for fun, I asked him to move to his left so that we could ultimately travel the length of the bridge with his back feet on the ground and his front feet on the bridge.

He moved sideways willingly, and as we approached the center of the bridge, the point at which it would tip, he began to slow down. He had slowed so much that he was barely moving as we crossed over the tipping point. Having just crossed the thing twice, he knew the bridge would tip, and it seemed as though he didn't want to surprise himself when it did. The interesting thing was that as his left front foot crossed the bridge's center, he placed it in such a way so that bridge began to balance ever so briefly, with both ends roughly an equal distance off the ground.

We hesitated there for a second before Smokey shifted his weight a little more to the left. The bridge slowly tipped in that direction, with the edge of the bridge gently landing on the ground before we continued on our way. As we side-passed around that end of the bridge, Smokey's front feet were still on the bridge and his hind feet were still on the ground. Once on the other side, we headed back the way we came.

As we approached the middle of the bridge, Smokey slowed. Again, he hesitated before stepping across the tipping point. This time, I sat quietly on his back allowing him to make the next move without any interruption from me. I felt him shift his weight slightly over the tipping point without moving his feet. The bridge didn't tip. He squared himself up, and then shifted his left front foot slightly. Again, the bridge didn't move. He stayed there for a few seconds, then leaving his foot in position on the bridge, ever-so-slowly began shifting his weight to the left, over the foot he had just placed. The bridge finally began to tip at the same speed he was shifting his weight.

It was then that something extraordinary happened. With both ends of the bridge now off the ground, albeit not an equal distance, I felt Smokey make tiny, and in some cases, almost imperceptible adjustments in how he was using his weight and balance. There was a slight tightening of a muscle in his shoulder, and almost simultaneously, a release in his back. Then just as quickly, the muscle in his shoulder loosened while he shifted a hind foot, followed by the seemingly insignificant tipping of his nose and the tightening of a muscle in his opposite shoulder.

With each of these small, incremental adjustments, the bridge would respond with tiny movements of its own. It would tip just a little to the left, and then slowly stop and drift back to the right before slowly stopping again and drifting back to the left. As Smokey's adjustments became smaller and smaller, the movement of the bridge grew ever more minutely fluid, until it seemed as though we were in a small boat on still water, with the only movement that of an almost undetectable rocking when a slight breeze passed over the water.

As I continued to sit quietly in the saddle, I began to feel the adjustments in Smokey's body go from what I might refer to as larger, "outside" adjustments—the tightening and loosening of relatively large muscles throughout his body—to internal adjustments. What I mean by that, and probably the best way for me to describe it, is that the adjustments seemed to be coming from somewhere deep inside him—almost as if they were just thoughts on his part. Or possibly the adjustments were coming from the very small, proprioceptive muscles deep inside the body, the ones that allow animals (including humans) to make nearly imperceptible adjustments in balance without having to engage larger muscle groups first.

Either way, within a very short time, and with very little, if any, guidance from me, Smokey had not only put himself in nearly perfect balance within himself, but had also managed to bring both ends of the teeter bridge an equal distance from the ground. He was then able to keep the bridge in that position for nearly thirty seconds. When I finally asked him to continue moving along the side of the bridge, it was with very little more than a thought on my part. Literally, almost as soon as I began thinking about moving, Smokey started shifting his weight in the direction of my thought.

The shift of his weight gently tipped the bridge in the direction of our travel, and as he shifted his weight a little more, the edge of the bridge very gently touched the ground, making no abrupt contact and no sound. Then, once the bridge had touched the ground, Smokey continued on his way as if what we had just done were the most natural thing in the world.

For me, however, the experience was a bit more remarkable. Put simply, it was the very first time I had physically, or perhaps more accurately, consciously, experienced the concept of kami-shitoe. Not necessarily the idea as it refers to the line between life and death, but rather as it might refer to the line between all things being available or nothing being available.

Most of the adjustments that Smokey made to get the bridge to balance had been so small that it was as if he were balancing on the edge of a very sharp knife blade. All I had to do was stay out of his way while he did it. And I think it was just sitting quietly and staying out of his way that allowed me to actually feel those tiny adjustments in the first place. Looking back, I'm fairly certain that had I been actively trying to help him, the things I might have done would have covered up that feel between the two of us and made his job that much more difficult.

For the rest of that day, and for many days that followed, I couldn't stop thinking about the extreme subtlety of what Smokey had done and how he had done it. It gave me pause to think about how much I must be missing in the communication my horses were offering during simple (and even not so simple) tasks we performed every day. It also caused me to start paying much closer attention to the things my horses were doing and offering while I was working with them, and to how I could either become a productive part of directing what they were offering, or needed to just step back and allow them to do the job they were being asked to do.

A month or so after Smokey and I were on the teeter bridge, I was riding another of my horses, Mouse, at one of our weeklong clinics. While waiting for the riders to get their horses ready for the day, Mouse and I approached the teeter bridge we had available for folks to work with. Mouse had crossed the bridge countless times and was an old hand at it. However, I had never taken the time to see if the two of us could get the thing to balance.

I decided that this was as good a time as any to give it a try, and I started Mouse over the bridge lengthwise. As we approached the center of the bridge, I asked him to stop. We stood quietly just this side of the tipping point and settled for a few seconds before I began thinking about asking him to move forward. Similarly to the way Smokey responded to roughly the same "internal" cue from me, Mouse began to shift his weight forward, toward the tipping point.

These types of responses from Mouse were not uncommon. Over the three years we had been together, we had developed a great connection and rapport, so much so that more times than not, just a thought on my part was all it would take to get him to respond. In fact, one day my assistant mentioned that when I was on Mouse, she never saw any physical aids from me, yet he still seemed to just do everything I was asking of him. I suggested she get on him so she could feel what he was like, and how little it took to get him to respond.

As soon as she stepped into the stirrup and settled into the saddle, her eyes grew wide.

"Oh my God!" she said. "I can feel him moving!"

She pointed down at the saddle horn and made a small circle with her finger.

"It's as if his insides are doing this!" She smiled. "He feels like he's saying I could go in any of these directions; all you have to do is pick one."

"Then pick one," I smiled.

She reached down and touched the reins without picking them up. She then began to turn her eyes to the left, and as she did, Mouse's head turned to the left and he began walking in that direction.

"Oh my God!" she repeated. "That's amazing! I've never felt a horse do that before."

Mouse was a truly a great horse. There was a willingness to him that made him an absolute joy to ride and work with, and while he sometimes found it difficult to trust certain people, strangers in particular, he would give you everything he had without question and without worry if he did. That was what he was doing that day on the bridge.

He stood, his weight shifted forward toward the tipping point but not willing to move unless I asked. It was clear we were going to need to take a small step in order to get the bridge moving, but instead of giving him a physical aid to ask him to move, I simply thought about how it would feel if it were I taking the step, and not him. I pictured myself taking a small step with my left foot. Within seconds, Mouse took the same size step forward.

He set his foot down right on the pivot of the bridge and almost before his foot had landed I was thinking about taking another step with my other foot. Again, he stepped forward with his other front foot. This time, the foot landed slightly past the pivot point, but not far enough to move the bridge.

Mouse and I continued to work this way for the next several minutes until finally, both his front feet and his hind feet were in position to get the bridge moving. All it would take would be the proper shifting of his weight to bring the low side of the bridge off the ground. We stood for a few seconds before I let out a deep breath and thought about us shifting forward. Before my thought was even completed, he was already doing it.

The low side of the bridge began to lift and as it did, I felt the same types of subtle adjustments in Mouse as I had in Smokey. There was a tightening of a muscle here, the loosening of one there, the slight tipping of his nose or raising or lowering of his head, or the gentle moving of a foot one way or another. Then, just like with Smokey, the adjustments grew smaller and smaller, until they seemed to be only on the inside of Mouse's body.

As Mouse was making those adjustments, I began to realize that I was making adjustments in my body as well. Each time an adjustment was made on his part, my body would seemingly counter it. In other words, if he adjusted to the right, I adjusted to the left. If he adjusted forward, I adjusted back. If he adjusted laterally forward to the right, I adjusted laterally backward to the left, and so on.

Now keep in mind that at this particular point in the exercise, the vast majority of these adjustments were not external movements by either one of us. Mostly they were the tiny, internal adjustments that would be very difficult for someone who was watching to see. As small as they were, however, they reminded me a little of a tree swaying in the wind. In order to stay upright, the top of the tree (me) might go one way while the bottom of the tree (Mouse) goes the other. Somewhere in the middle of all that seemingly extraneous movement, balance is achieved.

At any rate, seconds later, Mouse and I were standing in the middle of the bridge in perfect balance, and with both ends of the bridge an equal distance from the ground. But unlike when Smokey and I balanced the bridge a month earlier, Mouse and I were able to remain in that balanced position for much longer than thirty seconds. In fact, as the riders began to bring their horses into the field several minutes later, Mouse and I were still standing there balanced in the middle of that bridge.

It was odd, but right after we got the bridge in balance, I felt as though our balance was fleeting and that we could lose it at almost any time. But the longer we stayed in that position, the more it seemed possible that we could have stayed there as long as we chose. As the minutes ticked by, staying in that state of balance seemed to become almost effortless for both of us. In fact, the bridge only came out of balance when all of the riders had come out into the field ready to go to work and I asked Mouse to move forward.

Again, like Smokey, as I asked Mouse to step forward, he did so in a most slow and thoughtful way. In doing so, the end of the bridge slowly tipped toward the ground, touching it softly and without the hard bump that it could have made had we just mindlessly stepped forward.

As I drove home from the clinic that evening, I began to realize that what I had learned with Mouse that day, as well as what I had learned from Smokey and the bridge he and I had been on, actually had very little to do with getting a teeter bridge to balance. Rather, what I had begun to understand was that the entire undertaking was really just an exercise on how to learn to work the edge of balance. The edge of balance, I have come to understand, is that point in horsemanship that is so fleeting and misunderstood that many of us simply overlook it, or worse yet, miss it altogether.

The edge is just that: a point of refinement, very much like that very sharp knife blade I mentioned earlier. It's the point at which both horse and rider know exactly what they are going to do next, but neither have completely committed to it yet. Ultimately, it's that moment in time, that hundredth or even thousandth of a second just before the commitment takes place, that allows both parties to momentarily perch on the edge of that blade. It is then the commitment, both internal and external (or lack thereof), that allows us to either achieve the response we are looking for or end up with a response that is often much less than what we want.

Shortly after Mouse and I worked together on the bridge, I began looking for the edge in other things we were doing. I quickly found that the precision of almost any movement we attempted was all about working the edge. If I wanted a stop, for instance, I could pick up the reins and ask for a stop, or I could put the feel of the stop I was looking for in my body first.

This was not through any physical movement on my part, such as leaning back in the saddle, changing my seat position, or thrusting my feet into the stirrups, as we sometimes see with riders. Rather, I would simply think about how the inside of my body would feel if I stopped, if I were on the ground by myself without my horse. In doing this, I could then feel Mouse getting ready to stop, which in turn would allow the two of us to achieve that edge of commitment. Then, a split second later, when I would actually commit to asking for the stop through either an internal or a physical aid (or both), the stop would invariably come through softly, quickly, and precisely.

The truth is, I think most horse folks have, at one time or another, experienced the type of precision in communication that I'm talking about here. But the experience is usually so fleeting that by the time we realize something has happened, we question whether it really did or not. By that time, both horse and rider are usually on to the next thing, and the feel we just experienced is quickly forgotten. On top of that, much of what has traditionally been taught in almost any horsemanship discipline does not usually place emphasis on the type of exactness that it takes to consistently feel when both horse and rider have reached that particular edge of communication. As a result, we don't learn how to look for it, and we certainly don't learn how to feel for it.

Nowhere is that lack of accuracy more prevalent than in much of the types of groundwork taught in horsemanship these days. For instance, when we are confronted with a horse who doesn't want to be caught, the prevailing perception is that we need to push or chase the horse so that not wanting to be caught becomes much more difficult than being caught. Eventually, after being chased for a while, the horse tires and allows the person to approach and catch it.

But what that particular perception doesn't allow for are the little signs that the horse was no doubt offering up long before it felt like it had to leave in the first place. A subtle change in expression, the slight tightening of the jaw, a tiny shift of weight, a muscle tensing, or any number of other little signals it was probably sending could have told the handler that the horse was already on that edge. These are all signals that tell us a horse might be getting ready to move, but hasn't yet committed to doing so. It's usually only after we ignore the signal(s) and push the horse off the edge that it feels it has no choice but to move.

In our defense, many times we simply don't see the signs; we haven't been taught to look for them, we overlook them because we don't think they mean anything, or we think they mean something other than what they actually do. And because of that, we end up wasting an opportunity for communication at the subtlest level. A level, by the way, that I believe most horses use to communicate with one another.

Several years ago, I had the opportunity to work with an unusually high number of horses that were deemed difficult to catch by their owners. All of them came to me within a couple of days of one another, over a thirty- or forty-day period. Until then, I had a pretty textbook way of working with horses that had trouble being caught: I made them run more than they wanted to. Once they got tired of running, I would spend time getting them to turn toward and "hook on" to me, and from there, work on the actual catching part of the process. Depending on the size of the enclosure, the method itself was usually fairly successful in relatively short periods of time, often no longer than a half hour or so.

However, because I was seeing so many horses in such a compressed period of time, I began noticing similarities in behavior in almost every horse. I also began to notice (almost by accident) that if a horse offered a certain behavior, such as the tightening of a muscle or tensing of a jaw, and I responded a certain way—say, with a shifting of my weight in a certain direction, or even exhaling at a certain time—I could either elicit the response I was looking for or get one I didn't want.

Over and over, I saw similarities in posture, behavior, and tension, and over and over, I experimented with behaviors of my own. In doing so, I quickly found that the majority of the horses I was working with didn't actually want to run when approached. More times than not, they were running because of the way I responded to what they were offering!

All of the little gestures and movements they presented meant something—if not to me, certainly to them. But because I was (in their minds) ignoring the gestures, I ended up effectively pushing them past the precarious edge they were perched on, and thus caused them to appear as though they didn't want to cooperate.

It was amazing how much more accommodating the horses seemed to become once I really began to pay attention to the small things they offered. Suddenly, instead of ignoring that slight change of expression or tensing of a muscle or glance in a certain direction, I found that if I responded with shift of weight or slightly different angle of my shoulder, or even changed the way I breathed, a horse who in the past may have felt like running, wouldn't. Instead, he or she might stand and wait, and eventually relax a little. Then, with another shift of weight or change of angle or slight step in this direction or that, the horse might quietly begin to respond in kind.

By the end of that particular forty days, I had a completely different approach to the way I was seeing and working with horses that were deemed "hard to catch." Don't get me wrong—there was still a lot of experimentation and a lot of trial-and-error on my part, but there was also a whole lot less running involved.

I began to talk about this communication edge when I taught clinics, and tried to explain it as well as I could while demonstrating various riding or groundwork techniques. Over time, a number of folks asked me to put together a groundwork DVD in which I could show these types of subtle exchanges while working with hard-to-catch horses. So a few years back, I did just that.

For the filming of the DVD, I wanted to find a horse that was really struggling with being caught, one that had been having an issue for quite a while and might show some of the unwanted behavior most folks face when they have a similar issue with their own horse. As luck would have it, a friend who ran a nearby ranch had such a horse. An Appaloosa gelding, he had been on the ranch for several years and had had been notoriously hard to catch that entire time.

The gelding had been so hard to catch that the day before I was to pick him up to take him to the location where we would be filming the DVD, my friend's ranch hands had to bring the entire ranch remuda off pasture just so they could get that one gelding into the catch pen. The hands were unable to catch him in the pen, so they herded him into a smaller, adjacent pen. Whey they couldn't catch him in there either, they herded him into yet a smaller pen. Eventually, they shuffled him into a twenty- by sixteen-foot bullpen, filled the water tank, threw him some hay, and left him there for me to pick up the next morning.

When I walked into the pen, he almost immediately began showing many of the subtle signs I'd learned to associate with a horse who wasn't interested in trying to get away, but thought running was what he was sup-posed to do. Nervous, jumpy, and more than a little cautious, he began look-ing for an escape route almost as soon as I opened the gate. As he began pacing the back wall of the pen, I stood by the gate and watched him.

He quickly went in one direction, got to the fence that made up the long side of the pen, ducked his head toward the back of the pen, and flipped himself around. After doubling back he headed the other way until he got to the other long fence, where he would duck and flip himself back the other direction.

I spent a little time watching him, noticing that not only was he moving with quite a bit of energy, but he was also doing it in a relatively mindless manner. In other words, he wasn't looking for a way to stop himself and he wasn't really even giving any thought whatsoever as to what I might want. He was moving and that was about it.

Of course, while the fact that he felt like he had to move when I entered the pen was certainly one aspect of the issue, it was actually the way he was moving that got my attention. The gelding was worried, very worried. Certainly more worried than the situation would have normally called for. In watching him as he paced first one way, then the other, it occurred to me that his problem wasn't so much that he didn't want to be caught, but rather, was more about how he felt when someone approached him. In other words, just someone getting close to him seemed to cause him to worry, and it was that worry that set him in motion.

He wouldn't look at me as he moved, keeping his head and eyes pointed toward the back of the pen as he walked and trotted along the back wall. Still, instinct wouldn't allow him to ignore me completely, and in spite of himself, one of his ears remained pointed in my direction at all times. I continued to watch him closely as he made several more very fast and seemingly thoughtless passes along the back wall before I finally saw what I was looking for.

He was giving me an opening. It was small, very small, but it was there. With his left side to me and just before he ducked his head and flipped himself back the other direction, his head would tip ever so slightly in my direction and his left eye would very briefly look back at me. It was his edge, the very thin line where communication with him was possible—or not.

I watched him for two more passes to make sure I was actually seeing what I thought I was seeing, and both times, he repeated the exact same behavior. He would tip his head slightly and turn his eye back. Then, in a heartbeat, he would duck his head and flip himself back the other direction. I watched him for two more passes to get the feel and timing I thought I'd need for what I was going to do. On the next pass, I moved.

As he approached the side fence with his left side toward me, I waited for the point just before he tipped his head in my direction, and as close as I could get to that moment, I shifted my weight slightly to my right. My shift coincided almost perfectly with his head tip, which in turn acted like a magnet that sort of pulled his gaze a little farther in my direction.

This change disrupted his movement for just a second, but not enough to stop him from ducking and heading back the other direction once again. On the next pass, the two of us did exactly the same thing. Just before he tipped his head, I shifted my weight and this time, his head turned even more, which actually caused him to stop his movement for just a second before ducking and turning. But it was the next pass that would do the trick.

As he neared the side fence with his left side toward me, I again shifted and again his head began turning toward me. This time, he not only locked his eyes on me as he turned his head, but at the same time, he actually stopped moving altogether. It seemed to surprise him a little, and he stood looking at me, his head high and eyes wide. He flared his nostrils and blew hard through his nose, making the kind of sound a horse uses to alert the herd or to ward off a potential predator. It was loud enough to bounce off the nearby barn and sheds and travel out into the valley below, where it echoed off the trees on the other side of the meadow and eventually returned.

He quickly raised and lowered his head, as though trying to judge the distance between us, while at the same time sizing me up to see what, if any, kind of threat I was. I shifted my weight to the right again, and his head bobbing immediately stopped. Keeping a wary eye on me, he slowly turned his head to the right, as if he were getting ready to duck and turn again, but one more right hand shift from me was all it took to bring his attention back in my direction.

As his head came around toward me, I once again shifted to my right, actually taking one very small step in that direction. The gelding almost instinctively followed suit. My movement had again coincided with the turning of his head, and for a second, it seemed that our movements were connected. As I moved, his head came around with my step, and his left front foot seemed to automatically follow his head. Then we were both still once again.

We had begun to work the edge, that small moment of communication where, simultaneously, everything is available and nothing is available. For the next few minutes, any move I made, no matter how slight, was immediately followed by a similarly slight move by the gelding. If I shifted to my right, he would shift to his left, toward me. The more time we spent on these simple, small movements, the more comfortable he seemed to become. Soon, I had turned the small movements into small steps, and then larger ones. Finally, I was quietly walking a small half circle around toward his hindquarters, and he was reciprocating by keeping his head facing me, and actually taking steps in my direction.

Seconds later, I slipped the halter over his nose, buckled it in place, and led him quietly from the pen. He loaded into the trailer without a problem and traveled quietly to where we would be filming the DVD. We had already discussed how we wanted to handle the filming, which was to begin with me off-loading the gelding at the venue and taking him directly to the round pen that we would be working in, which is what we did.

The rest of the work we did with him was basically filmed in real time. The problem, if you want to call it that, was that the little work that we had just done at the ranch almost immediately transferred to the round pen. So instead of the gelding looking like the chronically hard-to-catch horse he had been up to that point, he actually started looking for a way to be with us almost right from the start!

He did make a couple of half-hearted attempts at moving away when I first entered the pen, and for a couple of seconds, I wondered if he would revert to the behavior he had exhibited before I picked him up that morning (which would have been good, I suppose, for the production value of the video, but not necessarily good for the horse). But he didn't. Within a very few minutes, he began to offer those small openings in his behavior that told us he didn't want to run. They were little more than things like a slight change in where he was looking, or a seemingly inconsequential tipping of the nose or release of tension in a muscle. But they were big enough to build on.

As the two of us worked, I made every attempt to try and catch the little signals that he was offering, and in some cases, anticipate them, offering very small movements or adjustments of my own. Again, these were little more than a shift of my weight one way or another, taking a step in a certain direction—forward, backward, or sideways—or the subtle tipping or turning of my body. Sometimes, it was raising or lowering my arm ever so slightly, or even inhaling or exhaling a certain way at a certain time.

These were all things I had learned to do over the years in situations like this, and, as mentioned earlier, I stumbled upon most of them by simple trial and error. But they helped me to sort of squeeze into the emotional area the gelding was presenting. I use the word "squeeze" here because in some cases, and for me, that is exactly what it feels like: gently squeezing through a very small slit in a curtain, and doing so without causing the curtain to part any more than it already is.

It can be a delicate balancing act at times, but when it's done properly, the horse can allow us into the opening, which leads to his emotional edge. Of course, getting to that edge with a horse is one thing. Kindly tending to it once there is quite another. And to be honest, it is the "kindly tending" part, not the getting to it part, that most folks struggle with.

Our propensity to want to get things done quickly; or perform a certain technique exactly as we have seen our favorite trainer, clinician, or instructor perform it; or get the exact response that we have been told we should be getting, often gets in our way. All of these things can, and often do, stifle our ability to experiment with feel and observation of the horse. I am talking about the inside of the horse here, not the outside. This is important because, at least in my experience, it is that experimentation that can, and often does, allow us to not only get to that edge each horse seems to have and wants to offer us, but also allows us to balance on it and influence it in a productive way.

Now I suppose some folks reading this may be thinking to themselves that they simply don't have the skills to work with a horse on such a fine line of emotional balance. I have to respectfully disagree. I think we all have not only the ability, but also the need, and even drive, to communicate at such a subtle level. After all, it is no doubt the level of communication we all had before humans had language, and even today, it is still the level we use to interpret emotions in other human beings, and even other animals, just by looking at them.

Working the edge is nothing new to the human race, and it is certainly nothing new to the animal world. The problem is, the edge many of us humans get stuck on is closer to the blunt edge of an axe, the side you might pound nails with, than it is to the very sharp edge of a highly honed knife blade.

But with time, patience (both with ourselves and with our horses), and ultimately, forgiveness for the fact that we just aren't going to get it right every time, even the blunt edge of that axe can be brought to a perfectly gleaming and sharpened edge. Once that happens, we could find ourselves being a little bit more like those young men driving down the road on their way to the ski slopes—the ones sporting a sticker on their bumper that read: "If you're living on the edge, you're taking up too much room"!

Cultivating Softness

Lasell Jaretzki Bartlett

Softness is what emerges when we don't need defenses. My primary work is with people who are defended to a point at which their family, school, work, health, recreation, and other relationships are impaired. I also work with people whose physical functioning is limited due to genetics and accidents.

Most of how I facilitate change in others is nonverbally through my presence, although my professional training and experience certainly includes verbal interventions. I use words to engage and guide experiential learning, and do my best to talk people out of their defenses. The goal of using words is to help someone find comfort in their internal world, where there are no words.

When I am soft in response to someone's defensiveness, it is disarming, and allows a person to explore new possibilities, new ways to connect relationally. Being soft is how I support others while they struggle in their learning process . . . where any urgency to relieve another's angst dissolves.

The more I cultivate softness in myself, the more effective I am in creating a safe environment where others, in their journey to wholeness, can uncover and recover and discover various parts of themselves.

I am also on a journey to wholeness myself, and to find softness, I have needed help from those who are further along. In turn, I want to share the softness I have found with anyone who seeks a way of being that is simpler, clearer, and richer in the most surprising ways.

Coming in contact with people who are living with relatively few and infrequent moments of defensiveness has been one of the greatest gifts in my life. Those relationships remind me that ever more softness is possible, and re-inspire me to continue my practice of developing softness. This gift is one that reaches deep inside, taking up residence in my core and eliciting changes that persist through time spent away from the influential sphere of those further along.

There is an element of "not knowing" at the core of softness. To be okay with not knowing is where curiosity and wonder arise. To be at ease with not knowing gives me access to new questions that I may offer others to aid their searching. These questions serve both to initiate an internal search and to make meaning of a search in progress.

Bringing curiosity and wonder to everyone I encounter helps me be present and responsive to myriad communications with others. It is how I can welcome and encourage the search for balance and vitality, and seems far more effective a motivation than attending exclusively to a person's symptoms of distress.

Being in softness allows deep breaths, deep calm, and deep connectedness. It's a choice I keep making.

Simplicity 7

I was on the road, listening to a football game between the Denver Broncos and the Dallas Cowboys on the radio as I drove. With less than two minutes left, and with the score tied at forty-eight, Dallas's quarterback threw an interception that gave Denver the ball in their own territory. A few plays later, with around one minute, thirty seconds left, it seemed as though the choice for the next play would be easy. Denver—with a first down on the one-yard line—would snap the ball and put it in the end zone for the go-ahead score.

I think most folks watching (or listening, in my case) thought that was what the Denver coaches would have their team do. Score the touchdown, then see if the defense could hold Dallas from scoring during the remaining minute and twenty-five or so seconds that would probably be left in the game. The problem was, Denver's defense had been having just as much trouble stopping the Dallas offense throughout the day as Dallas had stopping Denver's. It would not have been out of the question to see Dallas march down the field and score a touchdown of their own. Still, Denver's choice did seem like a pretty easy one. Score, then try to hold.

The Denver coaches, however, had a much simpler solution. Let the quarterback take the snap, drop back a few yards, and fall down, stopping the play but keeping the clock running. On the next snap, that's what he did, and he did the same on the snap after that. In doing so, the Denver Broncos used up all but two seconds on the clock, which then allowed their field goal kicker to come on the field and kick the winning field goal with no time left for Dallas to come back and score.

It was a simple solution, when the easy solution would have seemed much more logical. Yet I believe what those coaches understood is that there is a big difference between doing something because it's simple, and doing something because it's easy.

In horsemanship, as in life, I suppose, we have a tendency to get the two concepts confused as well. We sometimes think that because we say something is easy, it automatically means it's simple, and because something is simple, it automatically means it's easy. But the truth is, more times than not, neither is actually the case.

I grew up working for the Old Man—Walter Pruit—a horseman who always kept things as simple as possible, not only when working with horses, but in pretty much everything he did. If he needed a horse to do something, he'd ask the horse to do it, and then he would make sure, as kindly as possible, that the horse followed through and did it. No fanfare, no emotion, no extraneous movement, and no big deal. If a horse were worried, he'd help calm it down. If a horse needed to bring up some energy, he'd help it do that, too. If a job needed to get done, any job, it got done.

Walter's tools were simple ones as well. He had a halter and lead rope for every horse on the place; most of the halters were leather, and the ropes were cotton or hemp. He had a pair of old batwing chaps that he wore from time to time, mostly when it was cold; a number of old, well-cared-for bridles with a variety of bits; and a pair of well-worn leather reins for each.

Also in his tack room were three twenty-five-foot-long battered and frayed cotton ropes that he used for lunge lines; four equally frayed thirty-five-foot-long cotton ropes he used for ground driving; a couple of old buggy whips; a bull whip; and four old saddles, three of which were built in the late 1800s (one was slightly newer, but not by much). He had three or four lariats and was a masterful hand with them, although I only saw him use them a handful of times.

Although these are the specific tools I remember seeing on the place or in his tack room, in looking back, I never really took much notice of which tools he used when he worked with a horse. For me, it wasn't the tools that made an impression on me, but rather the fluidity of his movements, what he did with his hands, the placement of his body in relation to the horse's body, the timing of his advance into a certain situation, or his retreat from another.

As I grew older and began taking jobs on various ranches, I carried with me that same simplicity in my own tools and how I used them. As I've mentioned, I had a fairly sheltered background when it came to my early work with horses. Other than the time I spent with Walter when I was young, I usually ended up on one relatively secluded ranch or another. Most of those outfits were pretty lenient as to what was done with the horses, or what was used to accomplish it, and so the meager tools I brought with me were never given any thought by those who hired me or those I worked with. Also, because I was normally the fellow in charge of the horse operations to begin with, and because we were fairly successful with our training practices on these outfits, there wasn't really any need to change or add to the tools we used.

But as time went on, and I entered the "real world" of horse training, I began to see that there were a lot of trainers out there using specialized and seemingly useful tools. A couple worth mentioning were lead ropes and halters made from yacht rope instead of cotton or leather (in the case of the halters); a small flag on the end of a stick or whip to help direct, move, or desensitize a horse; and lariats for working horses in all types of situations, from catching them (by roping them) to roping a foot to teach them how to be led by their feet (instead of, or in addition to, a head halter).

Because I had been so sheltered up until then, when I saw tools like these used for the first time, it was as though a whole new world of training opened up for me. I almost immediately fashioned myself a flag by placing a brown paper sack inside a small plastic grocery bag and duct-taping it to the end of an old whip. I also began finding other uses for my lariats, which up until then, I had only used when working cattle.

Soon, I was using the flag I had made to help load horses in trailers, desensitize young or nervous horses, move horses from one pen to another, or sort others from a herd. I began roping the feet of young horses during the starting process, something I hadn't really seen the need to do in the past. But because I had read an article on how roping a horse's feet could get the horse ready to be hobbled or learn not to panic should it get hung up in a fence, it suddenly seemed a pretty important thing to do. It seemed so important, not to mention logical, that over the course of a few weeks, every horse on the place had his or her feet roped and messed with on at least a few occasions.

As time went on, I began seeing and hearing about certain training techniques that I hadn't used, but that sounded as if they might be a good idea. There were techniques such as laying down an unruly horse so that the horse could learn how to submit and relax, or performing one-rein stops over and over so that a horse learned how to disengage its hindquarters in an emergency situation. There was also getting a horse to give laterally to the bit, again, over and over, so that it could learn to become supple through its neck and body.

On the ground, time was spent teaching horses how to yield their fore-hands and hindquarters, how to sidepass and back up—almost all of which was taught by swinging or shaking a lead rope (as I had seen folks do) in order to get the desired response. I dabbled in bridleless and bareback riding because I'd heard that it was a good way to see if you had a solid relationship with your horse, and I began starting horses in small groups instead of one at a time because I'd heard that was an easier and quicker way to do it.

An associate mentioned that almost everything is easier when work-ing horses if you do it from the back of another horse. So I thought I'd give that a try, too. For the next couple of years, much of the work I did with the horses on the ranch was performed while I was on my horse Buck, or another horse we had on the place, Biggie.

Now I must say that while I certainly enjoyed all of the work I did during that period in my life, and while admittedly I also learned a great deal during that time, not to mention developed or honed certain useful skills, today I look back and sort of jokingly refer to it as my "lost years." Lost because in my quest to find easier, more efficient, or better ways to do things, I strayed further and further from what I consider to be my horse-training roots.

In the past, those roots had always been based on developing simplic-ity of communication with the horse, not necessarily on ease of technique. What I mean by that is, for instance, using a flag to help move a horse out of our personal space may be a relatively easy way to accomplish the goal, but it isn't necessarily simple. Simple would be helping the horse understand how to move out of that space just by seeing or feeling a certain movement or energy in our body. Having to retrieve the flag, carry the flag, then use the flag to accomplish the same goal isn't simple.

I suppose it's similar to the idea that the shortest distance between two points is a straight line. In other words, why add steps to a process that can be made much simpler? Before going any further, I must stress that what I am saying here is in no way a criticism of anybody who uses any of the tools or techniques that I mentioned above. In fact, this really has nothing to do with anybody else, what they do, or how they do it. It has to do with my own journey and the things that I've found important to the goals that I am hoping to achieve someday.

For me, the goal of becoming a horseman has much less to do with tools and aids than it does with the refinement of self. It seems to me that with self-refinement not only will the tools and aids we use not matter so much, but the number of tools and aids we use won't matter that much either.

At a clinic not long ago, I had an opportunity to work with a rider who was hoping to move her horse into First Level dressage. However, the two of them were struggling with a couple of required movements, not the least of which was having a clean leg-yield. As the rider and I visited about the things she wanted to work on during her session, I asked her what aids she was currently using to help get the leg-yield from her horse.

The woman sat up in the saddle, looked straight ahead, and began reciting a litany of steps.

"I use a slightly increased pushing pressure with my lower leg and seat bone on the same side," the woman said. "I sit slightly heavier on the inside seat bone, with my inside leg just behind the girth. Doing that should push the hindquarters forward and sideways at the same time."

"Okay. . . " I started.

"I apply that aid at the moment when the inside hind leg is lifted off the ground to start a forward-sideways step," she continued. "I also put my outside leg in a guarding position behind the girth, blocking her from moving her quarters too far sideways and maintaining the forward movement at the same time."

"I see."

"My inside leg drives, while the outside leg controls." She hesitated for a second, as if trying to remember the rest. "I guide the forehand along the wall with the outside rein. By supporting with the outside leg, I should be able to keep her from rushing away from the inside leg. The supporting outside rein prevents any falling out over the outside shoulder."

I waited this time to see if there was more. There was.

"Ultimately, I'm trying to get her to be flexed away from the direction we are moving and her forehand guided in a shallow turn to align with the hindquarters." She finally turned and looked back down at me. "Her inside legs should pass and cross in front of her outside legs." She smiled.

"Okay." I nodded. "And how are you both doing with all of that?"

"Not very well."

"Fair enough." I nodded again. "So let's try something a little different."

"Okay."

"Let's take her down to the end of the arena at the trot," I started. "When you get to the far end, bring her back this direction down the middle of the arena. When you want her to start her leg-yield, all I want you to do is, when her right hind foot leaves the ground, just start thinking about that foot traveling under her body and landing under your left foot."

"At a trot?" she questioned.

"Yes, a trot. It might be easier for her if she has a little momentum."

"No leg aid?"

"Not if you can help it."

"Okay." She sounded unsure. She trotted her mare to the other end of the arena and as requested, turned back down the middle of the pen and came back toward me. Within a few strides of getting the mare straight, the pair effortlessly began to drift sideways to the left, the direction of the leg-yield.

"Wow," the woman beamed. "She's doing it! And I'm not using any leg at all!"

"There you go," I said as she rode up. "Simple."

"Yeah." She was still smiling. "But it wasn't easy."

"I didn't say it would be." I shrugged. "But I bet if you do it a few more times, it will be."

Within twenty minutes, the two of them were effortlessly doing beautiful leg yields in both directions without the rider applying any noticeable leg pressure whatsoever.

In this case, it wasn't so much the tools that were getting in the way of communication between horse and rider as it was the number of aids that were being used, and which the rider needed to keep track of. For me, using that many aids to accomplish one thing is like wanting to put a nail in a board. We have the nail and we have the board. Now all we need is a tool to connect the two.

My choice would probably be a hammer. That, along with the skill to use it properly, would get the nail in the board as simply and efficiently as possible. I would probably not chose a hammer with a wrench attached to the handle, and a pliers holding the wrench, with a magnet to hold the nail upright and a clamp to hold the magnet in place, with two teenagers holding the clamp. Of course, none of that would be simple or easy, but you probably get the point.

This propensity to want to complicate things when it comes to horsemanship is nothing new. It's been going on for quite a while, and more often than not, folks who have been taught how to complicate things are the very ones who end up perpetuating it. But I think more than that, sometimes complicating things is also a way for an instructor to show a student just how much subject knowledge they have. Again, that is not a criticism, but rather an observation, and to be honest, I'm not sure anybody is immune to it.

I recall years ago, when I first began doing clinics, a student came to me wanting to know how to do a turn on the haunches with her horse. At the time, I was new in the clinic business and was getting a lot of people at my clinics, auditors mostly, who seemed to be attending just to question why I wasn't doing the work similar to the way other clinicians did theirs. During that time, I found that my "simple" explanations of certain movements or tasks were met with raised eyebrows and sometimes even downright disbelief. Disbelief in that the way I would describe something would be so basic that folks couldn't see how it could possibly work, even though we had proven that it would time and time again.

As a result, I found myself sometimes trying to make my explanations of things a bit more complicated than they actually needed to be. So when the student at this particular clinic asked about teaching her horse how to do a turn-on-the-haunches, my explanation came out in such a long and convoluted way that by the time I was finished, even I didn't understand it!

The student, to her credit, listened quietly as I presented all of the information, most of which was useless, and waited until I was finished before she meekly said, "I don't think I could do that."

I stood for a few seconds, trying to remember all that I had said, before looking up at her. "I don't think I could either," I said, and the folks in the audience let out a chuckle that sounded as if they were relieved to hear it, as well.

"So let's do this instead," I smiled. "Ask your horse to rock back on his hindquarters a little, and then when he does, gently lay the right rein on his neck and see what happens." The woman did exactly what I suggested, and her horse did one of the prettiest turns-on-the-haunches that I had ever seen. Simple.

I learned a very valuable lesson that day: people don't care how much you know, they care about whether or not you can help them and their horse. Condensing the information that is being presented and keeping it specific to the task at hand (whether we're teaching horses or people) is really the key to keeping things understandable, which in turn helps create relative ease in achievability. It is the ease of achievability that allows for quiet learning.

That isn't to say that there aren't times when the circumstances we are presented with simply won't allow (at least initially) quiet learning. Sometimes a traumatic background, for instance, may cause a horse to want to resist. Sometimes we may be trying to change or alter an unwanted learned behavior that is so strongly ingrained that the horse doesn't think it can change it. Other times, physical issues or ill-fitting tack may cause a horse to become defensive or overly reactive to even the simplest of requests, and still other times, a deeply held fear of something like crossing water or getting in a trailer will override the horse's ability to think its way through a situation.

These are all things that, at one time or another, I believe most horse folks (myself included) have been confronted with. Usually, the amount of success we achieve in getting horses like this to feel better can be directly correlated to how simply we can frame our request, how consistent we can be with that request, and how willing the horse is to change. Sometimes all of those things line up, and sometimes they don't. It is when they don't line up that we usually learn the most from them, about them, and most importantly, about ourselves.

Still, I can look back over the years and see that in almost every case when things didn't go very well during a training session, it was usually because I had abandoned simplicity. In every one of those cases, I can vividly recall the point at which I had let the situation get more complicated than it should have been. Every time that happened, things escalated, emotions began to run high, and quiet learning went right out the window.

In comparison, I recall that when I worked for the Old Man, for the most part, things around his place were always very calm and quiet. Part of that, I'm sure, had to do with the fact that he was fairly unflappable in general, and as such, very little seemed to bother him. Or at least if something did bother him, I never knew about it. But even more than that, as I get older, I am also beginning to understand that a big part of the quietness on his place also had to do with simplicity. There is quiet in simplicity, and he always kept things simple.

Other than those few years of experimentation—during which admittedly my training methods became pretty convoluted—I, too, have relied primarily on keeping things as simple as possible, and therefore as quiet as possible. I'm not sure that doing so was a conscious decision on my part, as much as it was just what has always felt right to me. Don't get me wrong. I'm not saying that those other methods, many of which work well for others, are necessarily bad, because they aren't. It's just that the feel of doing something with the least amount of effort, energy, and equipment has always resonated with me. I'm not sure if that's because it is what I sort of grew up with all those years ago working for Walter, or if it is just the nature I was born with. Either way, it resonates with me.

Some time back, I was having a conversation with someone at a clinic about my time with Walter. The person asked if the work I do with horses today is an attempt at trying to fill his shoes. It was an interesting question and one I had never given any thought to. However, after thinking about it for a few minutes, the answer I settled on was no. You see, there is no need to fill Walter's shoes, because they have already been filled once. There is no need to fill them again.

Of course, that doesn't mean that the kind of work that I do today, that quest for quiet simplicity, isn't in honor of my teacher from long ago, because it most certainly is. That is a given. Still, the thing that he instilled in me, probably without even knowing it, was that, while he gave me the "shoes" I wear today and put me on the path that I'm currently on, it is ultimately my responsibility to fill my own shoes, just as it is my responsibility to stay on my own path.

And I suppose in the end, it's just that simple . . . it's just not always that easy.

"Feel" Is a Verb

Tim Harvey

Feel," as I live it and experience it within my horsemanship, is a verb, not a noun. It is a way of communicating and participating in a two-way conversation. It is about sending as much as it is about receiving. I hear horsemen and trainers refer to feel all the time as though you can just reach out and grab it from your horse. I hear the catch phrases often. "Pick up a feel!" "Feel of your horse . . . now, feel with your horse!" It is often spoken of but rarely, if ever, described and, with few exceptions, never truly taught. I think the reason you do not hear descriptions of feel very often is simple. True feel is a very personal experience, and I think how it is accessed differs widely from person to person.

There are layers and stages to achieving feel with a horse. To me, feel has five layers or components: physical, mental, energetic, emotional, and spiritual. Each layer has benefits and advantages, and I aspire to operate within all five layers simultaneously when I am in the company of my horse.

The physical manifestation we pursue within our horsemanship is a result of achieving feel on these levels. It centers on and is all about the anticipation of a communication. It is defined as that moment when you realize that you don't have to say the next thing; your partner already gets it and you simply move on to the next movement.

It's allowing the flow of ideas and energy through the smoothest path by not impeding it, and doing so with the least amount of effort and information possible. No clutter. No ripples or splashes, not even a gurgle. Softening not just your hands, but also your eyes, your heart, and your entire being. Opening up to accept and consider offers that come your way. Not dictating how things will be, but embracing the concept that feel is a two-way street and your partner may have a better way of getting there. Feel is not just something you do to your horse but with your partner.

It is a dance where the partners glide across the floor quietly, softly entwined and so connected that it is difficult to say where one stops and the other begins. It is about trusting that your partner already knows what's next. That you do not need to tell, but instead suggest or ask. Then stay out of the way and go with your partner as a team. It means that sometimes you lead and sometimes you follow. The transitions between leading and following are seamless, quiet, and soft. It is about listening with not just your ears, but also with your heart and your spirit. Answering your partner from that secret spot within yourself that you are sometimes afraid to journey to yourself. Trusting that spot. Opening that spot to your partner. That is where true feel lies. It is where the spring of softness bubbles up. Allow it to flow and not only will your horsemanship change, but so will your life.

When I think back on my life and consider my vocations as well as avocations, I realize that I have always been most comfortable when relating to the world from a feeling level. As a child, I gravitated to pastimes and activities that accentuated feel. As I matured, the sports I participated in were singular rather than team-based, and a strong feel component was required in order to excel at them. A very competitive swimmer, I set state records in several events as a teen. The fine nuances required to beat my competitors were determined by my ability to feel my way through the water with the least amount of resistance and the maximum amount of speed. I remember experimenting with different breathing patterns, hand positions, and mental approaches while swimming.

I would meditate as I swam, centering my thoughts on the feel of the water flowing past different parts of my body. Realizing I could feel the resistance as well as the smoothness to different approaches. Finding that fine line and being able to perform strongly yet softly was key to winning. I found I liked to win. I had discovered the physical and energetic components to feel!

I started racing motorcycles as a teenager in the late sixties. I first started racing in Hare Scrambles and then motocross. I graduated to Enduro, or cross-country riding, and then to road racing. To an outsider, it looks like you are slamming your way around the track, but in reality, it takes a great deal of finesse to navigate the rough terrain at top speed while avoiding your fellow racers. The best and most efficient point of power is when your back wheel is just starting to break traction. Too much power and your wheel spins and you throw away the power you are looking for. Too little, and you bog down and fall behind. Feeling that fine edge, finding the breaking point, and being comfortable on the edge just before the break are the most important components. To some, it may seem like the edge of disaster. But when done from a feel perspective, it is intoxicating.

When I started road racing, the increase in speed made the ability to act without processing—ride by feel—much more critical to success. Unless you can live there comfortably, you are just out riding the track, not racing. The only way to be comfortable there is to be able to trust your sense of feel. Spend enough time there to recognize when you have arrived, and try not to think about it too much. I came to understand that feel can be lost by trying to find it in your head. Concentration can be an enemy. I learned to trust my own intuition and the importance of accepting the results of my decisions without second thoughts or analytical processes. I added the mental component of feel to my toolbox.

For most of my adult life, I have made my living as a carpenter and a sailor. Though they may seem disparate vocations, the two are bonded by the common element of feel. I learned my carpentry skills while working on wooden boats. You do not use squares and levels as in house building. Though tools are important, in boatbuilding, feel is an integral part of the process. Everything is relative to something else. As my mentor Richie told me early on, "If it looks good, it is. If it feels good, it's better." I learned to feel my way through a piece of wood. I selected wood for a project based on how I envisioned using it. I felt the grain and touched the surface to determine if it would bend fairly without crooks or splits. Picked it up in the middle to see if it was balanced and the density was consistent. There were times I selected or rejected a piece of wood simply by how it felt in my hands. I made decisions using an intangible process that was unique to my perspective and was based on my feel of the factors involved.

I am lucky that I had a mentor who never criticized my decisions. He encouraged and allowed me to learn at a level few others get a chance to experience. When I was right, my work was the best; when I was wrong, it was still good. I learned from my mistakes but I learned more from trusting the feel of what I was doing. This reinforced the physical, mental, and energetic components of feel. I was more and more aware that I was onto something that would affect my life profoundly.

I have over 80,000 miles at sea. Mostly on sailboats. When I think of how important feel is in sailing, I cannot understand how one could sail without it. Everything you do to move a boat with wind is based on feel. I learned to sail on a sixteen-foot boat. A boat that small transmits messages quickly and efficiently. It was a wonderful learning platform. You can feel every puff and lull in the wind. Feel the shifts in the wind. Feel the hull as it rises with every wave and bows into each trough. Feel the shudder of the hull when it slams into a wave face and feel it plane and lift as you surf down the backside. Feel the water slipping past the tiller in your hand as you slice through it.

If your sail is trimmed well, there is little weather helm or resistance. It feels as though you are flying, and the boat wants to go where you point it. It feels as though your boat is being lifted by an invisible hand into the wind. It's exhilarating! Conversely, if your sails are too hard or too soft, there is a heaviness and resistance in your hands instead. The sail looks and feels flat, or flaps. The wind coming off the sail is turbulent and erratic. The boat feels like it is working rather than flying. It feels like it is searching instead of determined to get somewhere.

When sailing, the direction of the wind is best ascertained by how it feels on your skin. Even though there are instruments nowadays that will give you this info, the best sailors are the ones who do not need or rely on instruments to steer their craft and trim their sails over the surface of the sea. They do it by feel. There is an intuitive feel to the process. The feel of the wind, the feel in the wheel or tiller, the rise and fall of the hull on the waves, the feel of the entire craft as it slices through the water or shudders when forced. All of these things and more combine into a single thing that is really two things: the feel of the craft and the feel of the sea. In moments of solitude at sea, I found myself overcome at times by the sense that I was close to discovering something about myself and about the world. But I could not quite see it. Like a movement in my peripheral view, if I looked directly at it or thought too hard, it would disappear. I found myself seeking the solitude and opportunities for introspection that being at sea provided. I was delving into the emotional side of feel. Unbeknownst to me at that time, the spiritual element was also tapping at my door.

I was around horses and mules as a youngster. My granny had mules on her farm in South Carolina. John, Granny's farmhand, could get those mules to do just about anything he wanted, and did it with a quiet ease that impressed even a ten-year-old boy. Kate was my favorite mule. Though she would not cooperate with most folks, especially Granny, she would do anything John needed done. She would pull a plow or cultivator, haul a wagonload of trash to the dump, stand quietly for hours in harness, and go straight to her stall when John told her, "Go to your room now, sweetie!" My favorite activity was when Kate would carry me and my cousin Eddy—bareback and bridleless—while following John around doing his chores.

One day I asked John, "How do you make Kate do what you want?"

To this day, my mental image of Santa Claus as he should be is John the moment he answered my question. Hands on his belly, head back laughing. Joy just flowing out of him.

"I don't make Kate do anything! I just ask her real nice. She does it because I don't tell her she has to."

I have often revisited that moment when in the company of my horses.

I rode horses on and off as I matured, and got very involved with them when I was in my thirties and raising four daughters—all of them horse-crazy. I bought them horses and naturally ended up doing a lot of their care. I decided that if I was going to do the work, I may as well ride, too, so I bought myself a horse. Doc was off-the-track and came with a lot of baggage! He was to be a first-rate teacher! He was an Appendix American Quarter Horse. He was sprint-raced until he was nine, and I got him as an eleven-year-old after a failed attempt by his previous owner to use him as a barrel racer. He had two speeds: on and off. He taught me a lot about feel right off the bat. It took very little to get him to go and a huge effort to get him to stop.

I began searching for a way to work with him that did not involve a new tack item or tool. I entered the emotional training program in a big way.

Doc helped me realize that feel was a two-way street. Until he came along, I thought I had pretty good feel. At a certain level, I did. I could feel a lot of things, and I had soft hands. But what I lacked was the emotional fitness connection link. I did not realize that sometimes feel was about something you could not physically touch. This realization was an epiphany, and very humbling. I spent many years with Doc. He took me places and introduced me to possibilities I never dreamed of. He prepared me for what was to come—my introduction to the spiritual element of feel.

I met Tico at a BLM facility in 2000. He is a Sulphur Springs Mustang with Sorraia bloodlines from Portugal that date back to the conquistadores and beyond. A warhorse. The kind of horse that chooses his human. That bonds with one person and doesn't allow another to even touch him. He came to me without a name, but I knew him the moment I saw him. For reasons that are too numerous to go into here, I named him Estrella Atlantico do Ponta Preta. Black Point Atlantic Star. Tico for short. My sensei had arrived!

Mark has written about Tico in some of his earlier books, so I will not go on about him here. Suffice it to say, Tico revealed to me the importance of the spiritual nature of feel. He also revealed to me that feel experienced on just one level is simply one part of what could be whole. To fully connect, to feel, you need to open up to the physical, energetic, mental, emotional, and spiritual nature of any and every interaction.

Tico taught me so much about what feel has become for me: The importance of not just being in the moment when it's convenient, but also living there as often as you can. Finding comfort in quiet, and acceptance of what is rather than frustration in what is not happening. Finding joy in what is offered in any given moment and working toward goals together, rather than simply having expectations. Listening rather than speaking, but speaking up when necessary. Recognizing that an intact spirit is so much more precious than an obedient servant.

Tico taught me to feel the quiet courage of trying something when your entire being tells you not to—trying because someone you trust has asked you to do this thing with him. The genuineness of truly feeling that "going with," and the bond it builds. He taught me to feel the joy in freedom, and that letting go with love can be the ultimate gift. That fear can be overcome and trust embraced. That courage isn't the absence of fear, but carrying on despite the fear. To feel that fear, recognize it, and overcome it brings peace. He taught me that to truly feel, I need to forget about what I expect to find, and instead, open myself to what is being offered; further, to accept that what is being offered is genuine and true. In return, I must strive to offer my best at all times. To be honest in my intentions because my horse already knows where I am coming from. Anything less than that dishonors the partnership. Tico taught me that without spirit, life is just an existence. He taught me that feel isn't about the weight in your hands; it's about the lightness in your heart. True feel requires more than one participant in the process. It is a language of a higher being.

So, what is feel? As I said in the beginning, it is a very personal journey. The experiences I had when racing motorcycles, sailing, and woodworking played a part in the development of what I now consider to be feel. They were missing a critical element however: a living, breathing partner, participating in a process of communication. Because of this, I think feel can mean different things to many people. To me, a quick definition must include the phrase "anticipation of a communication." What I have discussed here is my definition of feel at this moment. Perhaps over time, I will discover one, two, or many more components. My definition may change.

Whatever that change may be, I feel certain in my heart that it will only become clearer and more comfortable. It is a state of being. It is not a technique. It is an enigma. It is not tactile, yet can be felt through your hands. You cannot pick it up, but it can slip through your fingers. It has a lot more to do with your heart than your hands, yet your hands are the first place that your horse will check to see if you have it. One thing I know for sure: the learning never ends.

I feel that more is yet to come.

Feel 8

My dad was a very talented multisport athlete. Within about a four-month period in the late 1940s, he played on a semi-pro basketball team that nearly beat the Harlem Globetrotters (that was back when the Globetrotters were still playing against real basketball teams) and also had a tryout with the New York Yankees as a second baseman. Unfortunately, just prior to his tryout with the Yankees, he had an emergency tonsillectomy; he spit up blood during the entire three days he was there, so they gave him a train ticket home and never called him back.

I remember watching him play the three league team sports that were common for amateur athletes in the town we grew up in: basketball, softball, and flag football. He was good in all three sports, but was really good in what he referred to as "his" games: basketball and softball.

He was pretty amazing to watch back then, especially when he played basketball. He had very quick hand speed, was fast on his feet, had amazing control and vision of the floor, and a beautiful shot from almost anywhere. I'm not sure how many times I watched him grab a defensive rebound, dribble down the court at full speed, then pull up and float the most perfect jump shot effortlessly into the basket at the other end of the court.

His shots would often seem to defy gravity. They would hang in the air far above the defenders' reach, and then suddenly drop through the hoop as if guided by some unseen force. Sometimes the ball would make a swishing sound as it passed through the net, sometimes it would make no sound at all. The same thing happened when he used the backboard to bank his shots into the net. Whereas many of the players' shots would career off the backboard, making a ringing or booming sound when they hit, Dad's bank shots almost never made any sound whatsoever.

In total contrast, however, was how he hit a ball with a bat when he played softball. Dad was what was known as a "power hitter," and during his softball career, hit monstrous home runs off every pitcher he faced. In fact, decades later, when Dad was inducted into the state's Softball Hall of Fame, one of the pitchers whom he had gone up against on numerous occasions (also an inductee for his record-setting strike-out percentage) took the podium and said that Dad was the only batter he actually feared. He then went on to say that not only could he not strike my father out, but also he knew that every time he pitched to him, there was better-than-average chance he would soon be standing and watching helplessly as the ball flew over the outfield fence.

It seemed amazing to me that the same man who could so gently float a basketball through a hoop could also generate that kind of massive power with a baseball bat. Then, as I grew older, he began to teach me the finer points of how to play the games, and I began to understand the difference.

In basketball, he used what he would refer to as "touch." That is, just the right amount of effort needed to send the ball the required distance and still get it through the target. "Touch," the way I understood it, was all about disciplining the mind and body.

For my dad, the development of "touch" began when he was a child. He would take socks that his mother had folded by putting them together and stuffing one inside the other, creating a small ball, and toss them into the small triangular opening between the open door and a wall. He told me he would sit for hours on his bed lobbing the balled-up socks over the top of the door and into the opening. He found that the harder he tossed them, the more he missed. The softer he tossed them, the more floated into the space. Success was all about self-control and practice.

As he grew older and began playing basketball with his friends out on the playground, he would use the same concept, floating the ball instead of pushing it, and found that it worked equally well. He took the concept to the basketball court in high school, and again into his days playing semi-pro ball. Even well into his sixties, he was still able to beat my brothers and me (all accomplished players) when playing us in a game of "horse" out on the driveway, shooting at the hoop hung on the garage.

In contrast, hitting a homerun on a baseball diamond was all about the focused use of power. He told me on many occasions that hitting home runs wasn't about hitting the ball hard; it was about hitting the ball correctly. And correctness had more to do with self-control than almost anything else. Certainly, technique and mechanics came into play, but even with good technique and mechanics, without the self-control and timing it takes to get the bat in the right place at the right time to make contact with the ball, the swing is just as likely to be a miss as it is a hit.

Of course, Dad didn't hit homeruns every time he went up to bat. Nobody does. But then again, he didn't strike out much either. In fact, in all the years I watched him play, which were many, I can't remember any pitcher ever striking him out. What I do remember, though, is the way he could place a ball in the field after he hit it. No matter what pitch was thrown, it seemed that if he wasn't hitting the ball out of the park, he was dropping it somewhere the opposing fielders couldn't get to it.

If the outfielders dropped back almost to the fence and then spread out, Dad dropped the ball just over the top of infielder's reach and in front of the outfielders for a base hit. If the outfielders moved toward the infield, he would drive the ball over their heads for a double or triple. If the outfield shifted right, he would hit left; if they shifted left, he would hit right. If the infield left a gap in their defense, he would drive it straight through the gap. If the infield dropped back, he would bunt. If they came up close, he would hit it over their heads.

He had total command of the field when he came up to bat, and most opposing teams knew it. He had the same kind of command on the basketball court. He seemed to know where everybody was, whether they were his own players or those on the other team. In fact, he seemed to be able to anticipate where people would be at any given time, which made stealing the ball from the opponent or making a pass to a teammate seem effortless for him.

His specialty, and something that always seemed to excite the crowd, was his "no-look" passes to a teammate. He would be driving down the court with defenders in front of him, look to his right, then throw a pass to his left. Oftentimes, he would throw the pass to an open spot on the court where no players from either team were at the time, but then, just as the ball would arrive where he tossed it, one of his teammates would suddenly just be there, receive the pass, and go in for an easy lay-up or jump shot.

After one such game, during which he made a number of his no-look passes, we were driving home in our big Oldsmobile, and I asked him how he knew where to put the ball without looking. He told me that he often didn't really know until he actually passed the ball. He said that things happened so quickly on the court for him that if he looked for people to see where they were, whether it was his teammates or members of the other team, he was almost always late with his passes. But if he could feel where his players were, or where they were going to be, the passes were easy.

He said it was the same when he played baseball. He could see where the opposing fielders were when he went to the plate, but he could also feel where they were going to be once the ball left his bat. At the time, I had difficulty understanding what he meant when he used the word feel to describe how he was able to know where to throw a pass or where the outfielders would be. This was because my limited understanding of the word feel conjured up a picture of physically touching something, which he obviously wasn't doing. As a result, it was difficult for me to understand how he could not only feel someone who was nowhere near him, but how he could feel where those people were going to go!

It would be years before I would understand this relatively abstract concept of feel, and it would be more years still before I could see the many applications of the concept when it came to horsemanship.

As I've mentioned, when discussing feel in relation to horsemanship, most of us automatically assume we are talking about the feel between us and the horse's face or mouth through a rein or rope. While this is certainly the most common meaning, it is in no way the only one. Another form of feel is the kind I think my dad used when he played basketball. It's the kind in which we innately sense the presence or even the intent of another individual, even though we may not be in direct contact with them.

When it comes to horses, I became aware of this manner of feel some time back while helping out a friend on the ranch he was managing. We had just finished up a day during which we had driven his cattle into the high country to their summer pasture. The drive took five hours one-way, and because we had gotten a late start that morning, by the time we were heading back, it was already late afternoon.

About halfway between the ranch and the pasture, there was an area owned by a neighboring rancher that had a fairly decent-sized catch pen with some good grass growing in it and a water tank that was always full. It was easily accessible for trailers, too. By the time we got there, our horses were starting to play out, so my friend called back to the ranch and instructed his help to come pick us up with the big stock trailer.

Because it would take the better part of an hour for the trailer to show up, we decided to pull the tack from our horses and turn them into the catch pen so they could eat, drink, and roll. There were five of us on the drive, and we'd all worked together in the past. However, because we were all on horses who were new to each other, we thought it prudent to keep an eye on them as we turned them loose in the pen.

As expected, the horses, all geldings, went into the pen, sniffed noses, squealed a bit, and then went about their business. A couple of them rolled in a dirt patch in the middle of the pen, one went to the water tank and took a long drink, and the others just went to munching on the dry grass. Within a few minutes, all had settled in and were spread out in the pen and grazing peacefully.

As I sat under a nearby tree and watched the horses, I suddenly noticed something. Chub, a big paint, and Rocket, a bay gelding, seemed to be having some kind of discussion. With their heads down and eating, Chub would glance in Rocket's direction, and Rocket, in turn, would move toward Chub. Chub would turn his nose away a bit, and Rocket would ever so slightly create a hair more space between them. If Rocket took a step forward, so did Chub. If Rocket moved sideways, so did Chub.

This went on for a while, with the pair moving in a relatively large circle around an imaginary center point, just like two prizefighters feeling each other out in the middle of a boxing ring. To casually watch them, you wouldn't think a thing about what they were doing. They were both quietly eating and outwardly, looked as though neither knew the other existed. But it was clear after watching them for some time that they were indeed very aware of one another.

I continued to watch the pair do their delicate little dance and noticed that Rocket's hindquarters were always turned just a little bit toward Chub's face, and Chub always kept his forehand turned just a little toward Rocket's hindquarters. If Chub changed the angle of his nose toward Rocket, Rocket would adjust his hindquarters accordingly. If Chub backed off slightly, so did Rocket.

It was truly amazing to watch. Other than the obvious forward and circular movement, the rest of what they were doing was extremely subtle. In fact, it was so subtle that it looked like most of their communication was done with little more than a glance this way or that. It was as if they were feeling for one another just through the movement of an eye. Then, the more I watched, the more I noticed that it wasn't just Chub and Rocket who were having this discussion, but rather, all of the horses in the pen were doing the exact same thing.

One might move an eye this way and get a response from the horse to his right. He might then move his eye that way and get a response from the horse on the left. They seemed to be feeling for one another, and maintaining their spacing through those glances.

It was then that I began to understand what my dad was talking about when he said he could feel the people around him on the basketball court. These horses were doing the same thing. They were feeling for one another without touching. But what was more important was that they weren't just sending that feel, like we might do if we were trying to navigate a dark room— arms stretched out in front of us as we shuffle our way forward. Rather, they were receiving that feel as well, like my dad mentioned he would do. In other words, my dad didn't say he was feeling for his opponents (as one might navigate that dark room) but that he was just feeling them, the way a radio receives a signal being sent from some far-away tower.

For me, this is the key to feel. It's not just about sending a certain energy to a horse through a rope or rein or whatever. It's also about being open to receiving the horse's energy back. Feel is a two-way street—an exchange of information, not just the sending of it.

After watching the geldings in the pen that day, I began to wonder about something that I had felt when I was around horses ever since I was a kid. Being around horses has had a very positive effect on me. I could be having a bad day, for instance, and go into a pen of horses and almost automatically feel better. Even though I have heard many horse people over the years say the same thing about how they feel when they are around horses, I never really gave much serious thought as to why that might be happening.

Then one afternoon during our week-long clinics a few years back, some of the clinic participants and I went to clean up the pen that held our little herd of six or so horses. The horses were all near the middle of the pen munching on the hay piles we had put out for them minutes earlier, and we were picking up manure on the outer edge, near the fence. It had been a long, hot day and the folks who were helping me clean were all fairly tired, and thus fairly quiet.

I was pretty tired, too, and as I moved along the outside of the herd while we cleaned, my feeling of fatigue was quite strong. However, as I moved inside the sort of broken circle that the horses formed as they stood at the various hay piles, I almost immediately began to feel better. That isn't to say that I wasn't still tired, because I was. But I felt better—lighter, or maybe more open.

As the folks who were helping me moved into the circle, they began talking and making jokes with one another. Each one also made his or her way to one of the horses and gave it a pat (as had I). As I moved out of the circle, the feeling of fatigue began to cover the lighter, more open feeling I had just experienced. The other folks also returned to being more quiet and subdued as they left the circle.

After everybody left that pen and moved on to the next one that needed cleaning, I once again made my way into the circle. Again, almost as soon as I moved in amongst the herd, that feeling of lightness began to show up. Keep in mind that what I'm talking about here wasn't some huge wave that comes crashing on to a beach, because that wasn't even close to what was happening. This was subtle. In fact, so subtle that had I not been so tired to begin with, and in a fairly relaxed frame of mind, I may not have even noticed it myself. After all, I had been around horses nearly all my life and had never really noticed it before!

Over the next couple of days, I made a point to really pay attention to the way I felt any time I was in amongst a group of horses; in each case, that sort of light openness seemed to show up. It got me to wondering if the reason people feel so good when they're around horses is because they are stepping into what might be a series of unseen connected lines between the horses, based on their feel for one another.

The picture that comes to mind when I say "unseen connected lines" is a large grove of aspen trees. When we look at the grove, we see individual trees all standing together. But what we don't see is that underground, all of the trees in the grove are connected by the same root system. So even though the trees look separate, in reality they are really one being.

Yet, when we enter the grove, we feel the coolness of the shade, we breathe in the scent trees give off, and we hear the rustling of the leaves as the breeze passes through them. In short, as we enter the grove, the grove also enters us. Of course, we can very effectively stop the grove from entering by simply turning inside ourselves and ignoring those sights, sounds, and smells. When that happens, the grove simply becomes a bunch of trees that we have to walk through to get where we're going.

The same goes for the feel that horses offer us. We can either choose to be closed and insensitive to what they send and mindlessly pass through them in order to do little more than get where we're going, or, by opening ourselves up a little and allowing them to become part of us, we can allow the feel they offer to come in.

I think we get so stuck in the idea that we have to be touching something in order to feel it that we don't allow ourselves the mental flexibility to understand that true feel isn't initiated with physical contact. It begins with an emotional refinement within ourselves. It is that refinement that allows us to be able to send our intention (which, in my mind, is what feel really boils down to) while at the same time allowing ourselves to receive incoming intention. For me, emotional refinement is nothing more or less than limiting ego. Don't get me wrong; a healthy ego is a good thing. It's one of the things that motivates us to be good at what we do, and strive to be better.

It's when ego gets in the way of growth that we start having a problem.

An ego that tells us the horse must accomplish a certain task, maneuver, or exercise at any and all costs is more than likely getting in the way of not only our own personal growth, but also our horse's growth. An ego that tells us that the horse should be listening to us while we are ignoring what the horse is trying to say is also getting in the way of growth. The truth of the matter is, I, like so many other horse folks out there, can speak from experience on that one.

So what true feel boils down to, at least in my opinion, is the art of paying attention, not only listening to what our horses are trying to say, but hearing them as well. It's the hearing part that ultimately fosters understanding, and the understanding that supports growth in communication. In the end, it is the growth in communication that allows for the exchange of intent through the feel, and it is the exchange of intent that allows for the development of a relationship.

And after all, isn't that the one thing most of us are looking for with our horses anyway?

Opening to Softness

Crissi McDonald

It has become increasingly clear to me that it's the relationship between horse and human that is primary, not the training. It's the bond of trust, and the depth of understanding (of the horses and who they are, as well as the horses' understanding of the job we're asking them to do) that creates an ease of partnership. It's the ability to first be willing to do (and be) ourselves what we are asking our horses to do (and be).

When we start to explore the idea of softness in all its layers and colors, what we find is that the closer we can keep our horses to their intrinsic nature (quiet, soft), the better things go for not only us, but for our horses as well. The better they feel physically, mentally, and emotionally, the better they get at doing what we request of them.

I would like to share some thoughts about softness, as well as a couple of stories that, for me, demonstrate the benefit of pursuing this art.

It was a cold day down in Camp Verde, Arizona. I was watching Mark give a clinic and noticed that he was riding a new horse. Rocky, a chestnut gelding, had been born and grown up on the same ranch for the first seven years of his life; he'd never left the place. It was the first time that Mark was riding him, and the horse looked as though he was going to bolt at any minute. His ears were straight up, as was his neck, and every muscle in his body was on alert, ready to go any direction, at any time, with very little notice.

When he walked, he was angular and stiff. When he stopped, he looked around constantly, with the whites of his eyes showing.

Over the course of the morning (and the next three days I was there), I watched as Mark made seemingly small adjustments with Rocky, consistently asking for the horse's head to come down, going from halt to walk to halt again and again and again. During lunch on the third day, Rocky, still fully saddled, carefully lay down while tied to the hitch rail, and took a nap.

Fast-forward to 2012:

It was our day off, and Mark and I decided to go on a trail ride. We were giving a series of clinics in Texas, and were staying on a beautiful property that had several nice trails to explore. While saddling our geldings, I could hear them breathing quietly as they stood, eyes half-closed, enjoying the approaching spring's warmth.

Mark was riding his new gelding, Cooper, which meant that Rocky and I got to spend time together again. Although I had ridden him consistently for a number of years, it had been months since I'd last seen, much less ridden him. He had become Mark's primary clinic horse, and usually went on the many trips that the life of an equine clinician (and the clinician's horse) requires.

Halfway through our ride, we decided to leave the road and go through the forest. I quickly found out that riding through a forest in East Texas is far different than riding through a forest near our home in the Rocky Mountains of Colorado. The forest floor was covered in a thick overgrowth of long grasses; vines; and dense, tangled shrubs. Mark and Cooper worked their way through this maze of plant growth. Underneath me, I could feel Rocky slowing down as he navigated the terrain. And then he stopped.

A wise and seasoned trail horse, Rocky doesn't usually stop without reason. I asked him to go forward, but it felt like his feet were caught. I looked down and saw a vine wrapped around his rear feet. As I asked him to back up, it followed us. I asked him to go forward, and he couldn't. We tried several other maneuvers, finally backing up again and pushing the vine away with his hind feet. Out in front of us, the vine popped and jumped through the undergrowth, but the circle of the vine was slowly enlarging. We turned left, then Rocky sat back on his hindquarters and walked out of the knot of vines.

What struck me afterward was that during the minute or so it took us to get out of the vines, Rocky was never stressed or worried. He remained calm, listened to instruction, and was willing to let me know which direction was more open than another. We resumed the trail ride as though nothing had happened (which, in truth, nothing had).

At the same time, it occurred to me that in the six years we've had Rocky, neither of us has worked him with ropes around his feet, or made any effort to "desensitize" him to things on his legs. We have, however, offered him everything we share with our clients and their horses: softness, consistency, reaching a quiet frame of mind, boundaries, and so forth. We've helped him reach and maintain a quiet frame of mind (a foundation of softness) so often and so consistently that he now lives there on his own, no matter the circumstances, weather, or environment.

I'm not implying that training isn't important, or the work people do with putting ropes around a horse's legs and feet isn't valuable. I'm not saying there is only one way to cultivate a relationship with a horse, or that other training methods out there are wrong.

However, as a species, we (people) tend to focus on one thing to the exclusion of anything else. This is very prevalent in horse training—as I suspect it is in any kind of animal training. We are so focused, to the point of inflexibility at times, on getting the horse to do something we think important that we lose sight of how the horse feels about what they are doing.

What I would like to offer is that if we were to place how our horses feel (achieving a calm, soft, state of being) during any given interaction above what we can get our horses to do, horsemanship would look very different. Who knows—we might look different, too.

The early fall day warmed my mare and me as I coached a horse and rider through a new skill they were practicing. It was the first day my horse was able to be still not only with her body, but inside of herself too. She was, after two months, becoming my partner in teaching—we could ride up to another horse and she was no longer defensive, and whether being ridden or standing tied was quiet. On this day, while teaching, I had been looking over my shoulder, watching the horse and rider. As I turned my head and looked straight, I saw it: the paint gelding who had been tied to a tree had worked himself out of his halter and was galloping across the arena, wide-eyed and straight for us.

When I met this little Arabian mare, her owners had run into some financial difficulties and were looking for a home for her. By the end of the clinic my husband and I were giving, and after working with her during that time, we decided she would be a good addition to our herd. I named her Breagh (Gaelic for "beautiful"), but called her Bree.

Mark and I (as well as our dogs and horses) travel across the country to give horsemanship clinics. Our horses, seasoned by the road, constantly changing surroundings, and every variation of weather, were used to their job. Bree, having not been exposed to this way of life in her seven years, was understandably worried. A lot. She wasn't easy to catch, didn't stand quietly when tied, and didn't do much of anything else quietly either. She was a nice horse, but not particularly soft; she was guarded around people and met each request with a response that was the opposite of what I was looking for.

Each morning, I would tie her to the trailer, groom her, saddle her, and take her to whatever arena we happened to find ourselves in that week. She moved, pawed, pinned her ears, and swished her tail. As the weeks went by, and we worked more often than not, I watched her become quieter. We went from taking forty-five minutes to groom and saddle (a long time during a long workday) to being able to catch, groom, and tack up in less than fifteen minutes. I went from being able to only put my foot in the stirrup to being able to ride her for short amounts of time, to finally being able to teach while riding. She went from walking away when I approached her, to meeting Mark and me at the gate and dropping her nose into the halter.

After two months, she was starting to take on the air of a horse who knew her job; she was easy to handle, her eye had softened, her face and body had relaxed, and I could do pretty much anything during our workday that was needed. It felt as though the softness I had been offering her had begun to take root and grow.

As the paint gelding came galloping toward us, I only had time to think, This could be interesting. *Though he was almost on us, Bree didn't tense. She picked up her head, pinned her ears, and threw her nose to the left. The gelding quickly swerved to his right, heading to the opposite end of the arena, and I resumed my teaching. Bree returned to standing with one hind leg cocked and her ears relaxed.*

This incident wasn't lost on me. And it wasn't the first time I had had such an experience before with a horse—one that makes you realize that the horse you're riding has actually saved you from either an unexpected situation or your own silly decision. It was, however, the first time it dawned on me that what had just happened was a result of the relationship Bree and I had been cultivating. While there had been a fair amount of what most of us would call "training," it was secondary. My primary focus, with every interaction she and I had, was that I give her the best of myself every time we were together, in the softest way possible. What could have been chaos (a frightened and galloping horse coming at us) turned into nothing more than a small incident. It's my belief that because we had put softness as our most important way of being, she was quiet enough to only do what was necessary to take care of that situation. Nothing more, nothing less. Only in a balanced state of mind can we achieve this kind of clarity: in any given situation, we respond with just the right amount of whatever is needed.

This experience has become a cornerstone in my understanding of just how much horses give people because of a strong relationship. Of just how deeply softness goes for both horse and rider, if we but choose to practice it.

My dearest hope is that in some small way these ripples will go out and soften the lives of us all.

Softness 9

We are all, to one degree or another, products of our past. As such, we have a tendency to see things through the prism of our own historical makeup, and it is that makeup that helps shape much of what we believe, how we think, and what we do. Those qualities, along with the personality we are born with and other information we pick up along the way, have a tendency to make up who we are.

I think it's safe to say that the principles and ideals that I try to adhere to today when it comes to what I do with horses were instilled in me at a very early age. But on the other side of the coin, I think it is also safe to say that back then, I didn't really fully understand all that was happening when it came to what I was seeing or experiencing, either.

The Old Man's little horse ranch had a certain feel, or energy, to it. It was a place where things were quiet the majority of the time, horses were settled and happy, and there was an overall atmosphere of calmness that could be felt almost as soon as you came up the driveway. As a kid, not having been on any other ranches, I just assumed that was how all ranches were, and had no idea that anything special was going on.

I didn't really understand that the things the Old Man did and how he did them—the intent, feel, and heart he put behind the work—was what created that calmness. Because there was never a whole lot of talk about what he did or why he did it, or a lot of instruction about how I should do things, I was left to observe him and his ways and assume the results were in direct correlation to the mechanics of his actions.

The problem was that as I went out on my own and started to work with horses (both for the public as well as the various ranches on which I spent time), I soon found that replication of the kind of quietness that I experienced on the Old Man's place, or with his horses, simply wasn't achievable by imitation alone. For a number of years, I worked with horses in the same way I had seen Walter do when he spent time with his. During those years, I achieved a modicum of success in helping the horses I came in contact with. Still, I knew something was missing.

Then, when I was in my late twenties, a horse showed up that would help me understand what that missing piece was. Max was an Arab gelding, and he came to me during a period when I was working primarily with what many folks refer to as "problem" horses. He had many of the typical issues that I saw in other horses I had been working with: difficult to catch; an unwillingness to be saddled and ridden; various issues once a rider was on his back; and various degrees of defensiveness, from threatening to kick when approached from behind to offering to bite when approached from the front.

I went about my business with him in much the same way I worked with all of the horses with similar characteristics. I had him checked out by a vet and a chiropractor to eliminate any physical problems, made sure the tack we were using fit properly, and had his feet taken care of in a way that was going to be most beneficial to him and the work we would be doing. Then I set to the business of "training."

To say this particular horse was resistant to pretty much anything I asked him to do would have be an understatement. Things I tried that had been successful for me with horses in the past didn't seem to have any affect on Max whatsoever. In fact, in many ways, it seemed as though he was getting worse. Of course, the worse he got, the more pressure I put on him, and myself, to get a change from him. The more pressure I put on him, the more he fought.

One day, after a particularly long and unproductive session, I turned him loose in his corral and walked away, dejected that yet another day had gone by without much, if any, progress. Some time later, I happened to glance over at him and noticed he was standing at the far end of the pen, away from his feed. He had rolled in the wet spot over by his water tank, the one that I had created earlier in the day when I dumped the tank to clean it, and his whole left side, the side facing me, was caked in mud. His head was hanging low and he had one hind foot cocked under himself.

He seemed quiet enough as he stood there, but any time a horse isn't paying attention to its feed, there is always the worry that it isn't feeling good. So I watched him for a while longer, making sure he wasn't colicking. Just as I had decided he was okay and was about to get ready to finish my chores, the gelding turned and looked at me.

People who know me know that I've never been a big one for anthropo-morphizing—putting human thoughts and emotions on animals. However, I have to say, the look on that gelding's face literally stopped me in my tracks. I'm not sure if it was because of how badly our session had gone, or the fact that he was caked with mud nearly from his head to his tail, or that he appeared so tired, or a combination of all three. But as he stood looking at me in the late afternoon sun, I could have sworn he was saying, You're just one more human who doesn't get it.

Nobody will ever know if that was what he was actually saying, or even thinking, for that matter. In the end, it doesn't really matter much. What did matter was that after seeing the exhaustion on his face as he stared straight at me, it was what I felt. It was a look that haunted me the rest of that day, and during the rest of what turned out to be a sleepless night. As I lay there tossing and turning until the wee hours, I ran through everything I had done with Max up to that point. For the life of me, I couldn't imagine why he wasn't coming around. By the time I finally fell asleep around three in the morning or so, I hadn't made a lot of progress in coming up with an answer.

A few hours later, however, I woke suddenly, a distant memory racing through my mind. In this particular recollection, however, there were no pic-tures or words or even people, only the awareness of a feeling. The feeling itself, clear and distinct, was one that I had experienced on many occasions, but not recently. It was a memory of the quiet calmness I used to feel when I was around the Old Man and his horses.

It was then I realized what had been missing in my work (and not just my work with Max, but my work overall): the quiet calmness that helps cre-ate the intangible in horsemanship, that elusive connection that we all seek.

It is a piece of the puzzle that doesn't exist when mechanics through imitation are used, and why I was having so much trouble getting through to Max. After all, I wasn't really taking Max into consideration. All I had been thinking about was getting him to change, not how he would feel about it, or even the feel I was putting into it.

It was a huge awakening for me, and it took me a little while to get my head wrapped around it. I decided not to work with Max that day, or the next day or the day after that. Instead, I took that time to slow myself down and take a long hard look at what I was doing, and more importantly, why I was doing it. It wasn't until the morning of the third day that I awoke from another restless sleep to an understanding that would shape my horsemanship from that point forward.

It was a simple idea, one I had missed when it came to what I had seen and experienced with the Old Man in the days of my childhood. For Walter, working with horses wasn't how he made his living; it was how he lived his life. Up until that moment, without realizing it, I had been doing just the opposite.

In the tack room a couple of hours later, I sat on a pile of saddle blankets and gave some very serious thought to how I was living my life, and how it might be affecting my horsemanship. As time passed, I found myself staring at a picture in a dusty frame hanging on the wall opposite me. The picture was just a bit crooked, jarred askew by a gust of wind that had twisted through the tackroom door a month or so earlier. It was a photo of me astride a big black horse by the name of Kat.

Kat had come to me a few years earlier in a state of mind very similar to Max's. With Kat, however, I had been able to elicit a change a couple of weeks after his arrival. Like Max, Kat was resistant and defensive, and had actually taken to bucking and rearing on occasion, especially when things didn't go the way he felt they should (or at least that was my take on it at the time). Also like Max, I saw fit to up the pressure when he did something that I assumed was blatant resistance, or when I felt he was acting out.

On that particular day, we began the session pretty much like every other session we had had up to that point, with me asking him to leave the barn and ride down to the arena, and him resisting and trying to get back to the barn. I had already spent several days trying to "coax" him away from the barn as nicely as I could, and had even taken to leading him to the arena on a couple of occasions. But two weeks had passed without much real progress, so I decided the time was right to just go ahead and draw the line. By the end of the day, I told myself, we would be riding away from the barn.

Within a couple of steps in the direction of the arena, Kat began to resist. When he did that, I responded by insisting that he move, and he resisted more. It was then that I became much more adamant. The storm that followed was not only unpleasant for both of us, but also lasted nearly an hour and a half. By the time it was finished, we were both drenched in sweat and worn out. But Kat now left the barn without hesitation, and as far as I was concerned, the means had justified the ends.

Kat's owner took the photo on the day she picked him up, and she sent the framed picture to me a couple weeks later. She was extremely happy with Kat's progress and was pleased with how well he was doing since she got him home. But on that day, as I sat on the blankets staring at the picture, it dawned on me that I never really felt right about what had happened between the two of us that day in front of the barn.

I could have, and should have, done better by him, and I knew it. A sudden wave of regret washed over me, and I found myself wishing I could apologize to him, or make it up to him in some way. But I couldn't. What was past was past and the realization that I would never get that time with him back was suddenly overwhelming.

I got up from the saddle blankets, walked over, and straightened the picture. As I stepped back to make sure it was level, the thought from earlier that morning once again crossed my mind. Working with horses wasn't how the Old Man made his living; it was how he lived his life. It was then that the fog that had been hovering around me for several days slowly began to clear.

I realized that the kind of work I was trying to do with horses had never really been defined in my own mind. Because of that, the work that I was doing with horses like Max and Kat ended up being a poor imitation of what I had seen when I was younger. Because I didn't understand what I had seen back then, my own work ended up lacking true purpose. Kind of like an arrow that's missing its fletching—the little feathers that help keep it on target once it leaves the bow. Sure, the arrow might head in the general direction it was aimed, but without those little feathers, the chances of it actually hitting the target, no matter how talented the archer, are pretty slim.

I spent the rest of that day mentally going over how I had been when I worked with horses up to that point, specifically, troubled horses. Then I started thinking about how I wanted to be with them. The difference between the two paths quickly became apparent. What I wanted in my own horsemanship was to be able to help horses in as quiet a way possible so that they could function as easily with me around or on them as they could when they were by themselves.

But what was actually happening on a fairly consistent basis was that, if things didn't go the way I thought they should (and in a timely manner), I would often escalate the pressure. Doing this was always successful to one degree or another, but in the meantime, both the horse and I would almost always end up sweaty, out of breath, and exhausted, standing in a pen with a lot of dust hanging in the air from all our extraneous movements. It was a far cry from working as quietly as possible and ending up with a horse who could perform as easily with me as it could on its own.

The day went on and I continued to mull over my situation. It became clear that it was time for me to move on. I needed to let go of the past and redirect my energies into something that was going to be more productive and help me reach my goal. By the time evening rolled around, I had come to understand that what I was searching for, in both my horses and myself, was that quiet calmness I had experienced when I was younger. What had also become apparent was that in order for me to achieve that quiet calm-ness, many things were going to have to change, not just in how I worked with horses, but more importantly, in how I lived my life.

As I began working with Max again the next morning, I did so with a fresh outlook and a different plan. I would pick one thing that he was strug-gling with and then work with him as softly as I could until I saw some kind of positive change. We started with catching; that was one of his major issues, and seeing as how we couldn't work on anything else unless I could catch him, it seemed appropriate.

I entered the pen and, as expected, he took off for the other end, head high and tail in the air. In the past, I would have spun the lead rope I was carrying and caused him to run harder (making the wrong thing difficult). But on this day, I slowly followed him as he ran. When he got to the far end of the pen, he turned and looked at me as I walked quietly toward him. I only made it to the middle of the pen before he snorted and took off running for the other end. I turned and walked in the direction he was heading.

He ran back and forth inside the pen a number of times, with me always turning and heading in the direction he was traveling without speeding up, twirling my rope, or trying to cut him off. Soon, he cut the distance he was running in half, then he cut it in half again; finally, he was moving in a small circle right near the gate, and I was standing in the middle of the circle. A few minutes after that, he let me walk up to him. I stroked his head, neck, and shoulder, and then left the pen.

A couple of hours later, I went into the pen again, and again, he took off running. This time, he allowed me to walk up and pet him after running for about half the time he had earlier. After doing so, I left the pen. An hour or so later, we repeated the whole thing. This time, he moved away a few feet, then stopped and let me approach.

As I petted him gently on his shoulder, he lowered his head and let out a big sigh. It was the first time since he arrived that he actually looked calm and quiet, and I realized as I was petting him that it was the first time in a long time that I felt calm and quiet, too.

From that point forward, I approached everything I did with him in the same gentle manner, and he responded each day by becoming more open and receptive to what I was trying to show him. By the time he went back to his owner a couple of months later, Max was a different horse. Things that once seemed impossible for him had become easy, and the defensiveness that had once been such a big part of his life was simply gone.

Max was a really good horse; there was no question about that. There was also no question that had I not changed what I was doing and how I was doing it, that good horse may never have come out. It was difficult for me to admit, but admit it I did, and that in turn allowed me to understand that the majority of Max's transformation had come from an almost accidental softening in my approach. That softening allowed him to quiet his mind and let his guard down long enough to think through what was being presented. That softening put me on the path that I still travel to this day.

Over thirty years have passed since I worked with Max and Kat. Both are long gone by now, I suppose. Still, I have them to thank for initiating my desire to find quiet and effective ways to work with horses through developing and honing softness within myself—thus allowing the possibility to pass that softness along to the horses, and the people, I come in contact with.

That quest for softness within myself has taken me to some incredible personal heights, and it has also brought me to some incredible personal lows. It has allowed me to grow considerably as a horse person (and as a person), while still allowing for the occasional lapse of judgment and misstep in decisions. Luckily, those lapses and missteps are few and far between these days, and just as luckily, I continue to learn from them.

The quest for softness has also taken me all over the world, introducing me to and allowing me to learn from some of the top equine professionals in their respective fields. It has allowed me the honor of learning from some of the top masters in the world of martial arts, as well.

Yet, that same quest has kept me on the road year after year doing horsemanship clinics, often away from home for weeks, even months, at a time. It has kept me from being present for many important days in my children's lives, from family and friends I love, and the place I really want to be.

Now, I find myself closer to sixty than to fifty. While the quest for softness within myself is just as strong as it ever was—perhaps even more so—I sometimes wonder if it was worth it. Then, out of the blue, I have a day like one I had recently.

In the middle of the clinic, I left the round pen we had been working in and headed toward the arena. My horses were tied to the pipe fence that made up the arena, standing in the shade cast by two large trees just outside the pen. On this particular trip, I was traveling with three horses: my main clinic horse, Rocky; his traveling companion and my number two horse, Cooper; and a third horse, Lilly.

Lilly was a pretty little mare I had picked up a couple years before as a sort of rehab project. Nine years old at the time, she had been used for reining and had also been used as a brood mare. From all accounts, the training she experienced during her time as a reining prospect was fairly rough, and as a result, she had some major trust issues, particularly when being ridden. She also had a couple of serious injuries, as was evident by the large scar on her right hind leg and another substantial scar on her right side.

After getting her home, I rode her a couple of times and had a student ride her a few more, but decided she needed some time off before we did anything else with her. Because winter was coming on and my time to work with her would be limited anyway, I turned her out on winter pasture with the herd and figured I'd get to her in the spring.

When springtime came, I brought her home with every intention of spending time with her. But again, my busy travel schedule got in the way. She ended up sitting out the entire year and ultimately, went back on winter pasture that fall without having been handled much. The following spring, after bringing her home from pasture, we carved out some time to begin working with her. Then, the day I planned to start, she reinjured her right hind leg, and training got pushed back yet again.

As fall rolled around, she was once again healthy and sound, and we finally began working with her. We ground-drove her a handful of times, and then I began riding her in open country. During the first couple of rides, I found that her fear nearly overwhelmed her. She was trying with everything she had to do what I asked, but could do none of it with any kind of relaxation. To make matters worse, I also found that she had a major issue with turning to the right. Anytime I asked her for a right-hand turn, no matter how large the turn or how softly I asked, she would stiffen her entire body and frantically throw herself into a right-hand spin.

Over the next several days with miles of country to ride in, Lilly and I, and my wife Crissi, who was riding Rocky, made our way into the desert. I spent that time allowing Lilly to expend her frantic energy in large circles, sometimes riding up to a half-mile away from Crissi and Rocky before making our way back in their direction. We also spent time helping her feel better about her right-hand turn, as well as her need to want to stampede toward the barn any time she thought we were heading back in that direction.

After the second day, Lilly began to let her guard down and relax a little. By the third ride, she could drop her head and relax on the way out, but still struggled a bit on the way back. By our sixth ride, coming back was beginning to feel better for her, and on our seventh ride, she found a way to walk, trot, and lope quietly. After that seventh ride, I had to go back out on the road for a couple of clinics in California but instead of leaving her home, I loaded her in the trailer with Rocky and Cooper and took her along.

Lilly's demeanor on the ground had begun to change considerably. She was becoming quiet and friendly, when in the past she was a bit pushy and defensive. She also had a propensity to rush frantically through gates almost any time she approached one, but by the time we reached California, she had stopped doing that as well.

Initially, in the arena, Lilly showed the same types of behaviors that she had shown out in the open. She was tight and worried, and the trouble with her right-hand turn had come back. But by handling her in the same manner I had when we were out in the desert and giving her some quiet direction she could understand, within minutes of our first arena ride, she was going around on a loose rein with her head down and body relaxed.

The morning of the fourth day of the six-day clinic, I went to catch my horses to get them ready for the day. I was pleasantly surprised to find Lilly greeting me at the gate. That same morning, I rode her while coaching a couple of riders, and she remained soft and quiet the entire time. As the temperature rose, I tied all three of our horses in the shade of the big trees.

The first horse after lunch was a three-year-old filly we were working in the round pen. Having finished the session with the filly and her owner, I left the pen and stopped to chat with an auditor who had a question about the filly. While we were talking, I glanced over at my horses. Rocky and Cooper were in full view, as they were standing between the two big trees, but I couldn't see Lilly, who was tied and standing behind the tree on the left. I turned my attention back to the fellow who had asked the question, and while I was talking, I heard a soft nicker behind me.

At first, I thought the greeting had come from Rocky, as he often nickers when he sees me, but as I turned, I realized it wasn't. What I saw instead was Lilly, peering out from behind the tree, ears perked and staring straight at me. She nickered again when she saw me looking at her. I finished my conversation with the man, walked to the arena, and slipped under the fence between Rocky and Lilly.

Rocky turned toward me, and I petted him gently on his forehead. I then turned toward Lilly and found that she was already reaching her nose toward me, gently touching my elbow. I reached up and stroked her softly on the forehead as well, and as I did, she let out a long, soft breath. After a few seconds, I went to Cooper to give him a pat as well, and as I did, Lilly almost inaudibly nickered again while reaching out for me with her nose. Smiling, I gave her another pat.

As I stood there in the shade of those trees, surrounded by my horses, I was momentarily transported. There was no clinic going on, I wasn't a thousand miles from home, and all the triumphs and mistakes I'd had with horses in the past were little more than distant memories.

A quiet calmness, the kind I experienced so often in my childhood, slowly drifted over me, and I couldn't help but smile. Was this journey worth it, this quest for softness that has now spanned three decades of my life? Lilly again reached for me with her nose, and again I stroked her forehead.

I realized then that the answer lay within the willing reach of that once-troubled little mare. It had been worth it to her, and perhaps that was all the answer I really needed. It was certainly an answer my heart could live with, and maybe in the end, that's what really matters.

Afterword:
An Exercise in Softness

In putting this project together, one of the things I wanted to do was include some kind of simple exercise on softness for readers. But I didn't want to just write an exercise down and hope folks would give it a try, because ultimately some would and some wouldn't. Rather, we wanted to include everybody who read the book or watched the accompanying dVD by the same name).

After careful thought, I finally settled on a relatively subtle exercise that everybody who read this book or watches the DVDs has already become part of. The exercise is indeed simple and; is aimed at the very heart of everything we've been discussing in regard too softness. In particular, it is about noticing the kind of effect little things we come in contact with on a daily basis have on us.

To that end, as we finished this book and prepared it for publication, I decided to allow for some minor flaws in the structure of the content of the two paragraphs you just read to remain (not the content itself—just the structure). Some of you may have noticed a few of these flaws as you read the above. If so, how did seeing the flaws make you feel? Were you able to overlook them and simply move on, or did seeing the flaw cause you to become bothered or troubled in some way? Did noticing the flaw cause you to want to bring it to someone's attention so that it could be fixed? Were you able to accept or ignore it and move on? Or did you find yourself distracted or perhaps even impatient?

You see, true softness is always a byproduct of the internal softness that we carry with us in our everyday lives. Internal softness begins with the development of our ability to remain emotionally balanced even when things around us seem a bit unbalanced.

And so, I wanted to offer you this small exercise—one in which the focus is on distinguishing the difference between those things that are truly important and need our attention, and those things that are only peripheral and have no real bearing on us, our situation, and in this case, our ability to learn.

My hope is that everybody who reads this book will be able to see this little exercise on internal softness for what it is—a quiet reminder borne out of kindness and caring, and passed along from one student of the horse to another.

I want to truly thank you for allowing me to become a small part of your own Journey to Softness.